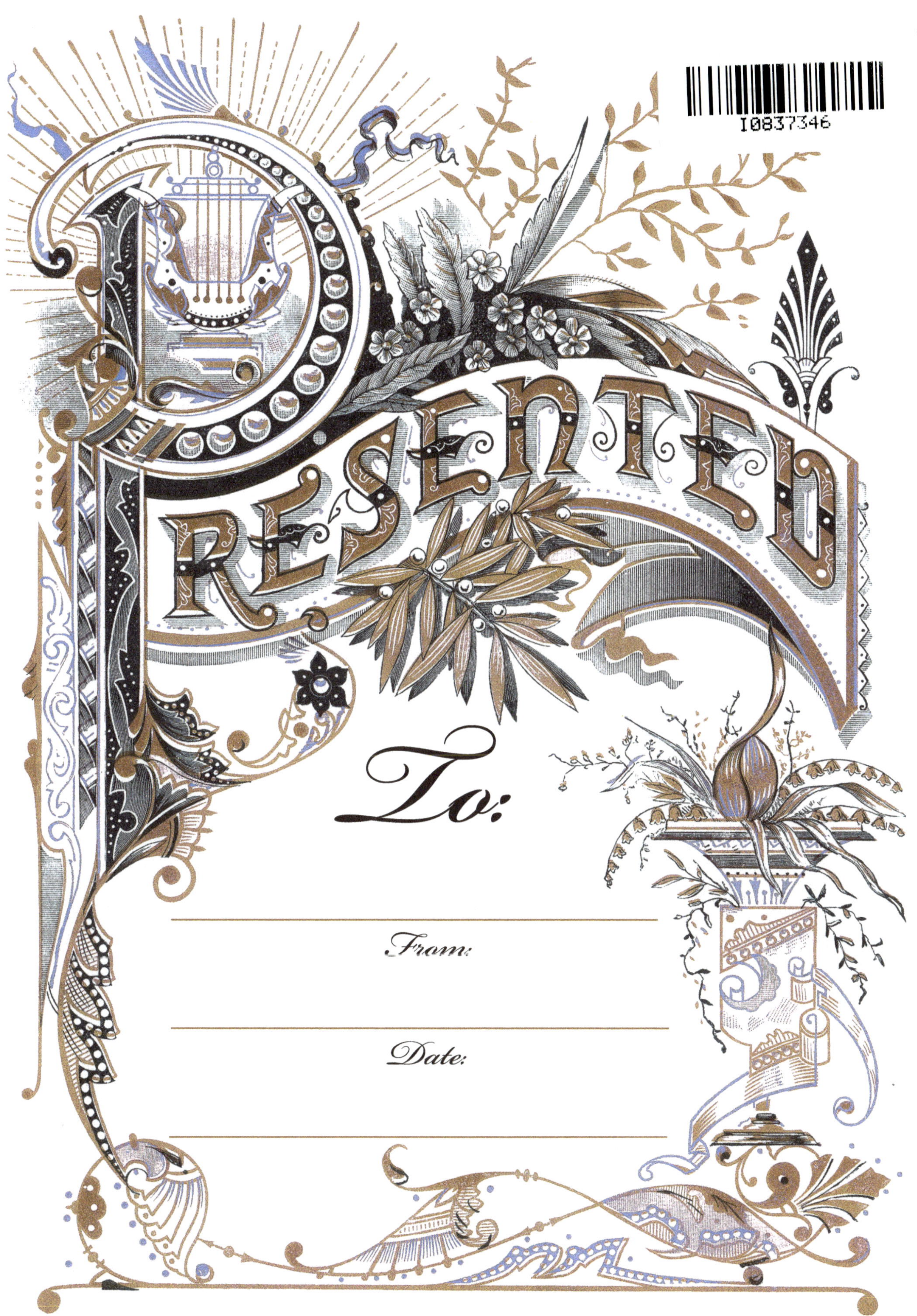

Presented
To:
From:
Date:

New Testament BIBLE STORY ILLUSTRATIONS

AN ADULT COLORING BOOK OF ANTIQUE ENGRAVINGS

LINDA WRIGHT

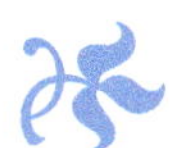

CLASSIC BOOKWRIGHTS
SANTA BARBARA, CALIFORNIA

Also by Classic Bookwrights:
Old Testament Bible Story Illustrations: An Adult Coloring Book of Antique Engravings by Linda Wright
Bible Stores for Children: Classic Bible Stories Every Child Should Know by Jesse Lyman Hurlbut
The Mary Frances Sewing Book 100th Anniversary Edition by Jane Eayre Fryer

Illustrations and Bible Stories are from
Charming Bible Stories by Henry Davenport Northrup, D.D.
with Sacred Allegories by Rev. William Adams
published by J.H.Moore, 1894 and
Mother Stories from the New Testament
by Howard E. Altemus published
by Henry Altemus Co., 1909.

This special collection of antique illustrations has been carefully restored with
state-of-the-art equipment and techniques for 21st century colorists.
Scanned, restored, edited and arranged by Linda Wright

Classic Bookwrights
P.O. Box 90135
Santa Barbara, California 93190
info@ClassicBookwrights.com

Version: 2.1

ISBN: 978-1-937564-09-4

Introduction

This book is a collection of beloved Bible stories as much as it is a coloring book. With artwork including the life of Christ, his teachings and miracles, his disciples, prophets and crucifixion, you can share in these recorded experiences and flood them with color while taking the opportunity for reflection. To enhance your enjoyment of coloring a page, each exquisite illustration is back-printed with an excerpt from the Bible story it depicts. Several sacred allegories provide further opportunity for quiet inspiration along with the creativity of coloring. Each page is printed on 70 lb. premium-weight paper that is acid free.

The drawings in this book have been shaded using the artistic techniques of hatching and cross-hatching. Simply color over these areas and allow the patterns below to show through. For further depth, additional shading can be applied on top. You may also find parts of certain drawings to be too detailed to color in every little area, so in that case, you may also choose to color over the top. For adding color, markers and colored pencils work well. For intricate details, try fine tip gel pens.

Test your media on a piece of scrap paper before starting on the artwork to be sure you are happy with the look. When coloring with pencils, start with a light touch. You can always go back and deepen the shade with more pressure and more layers but it's not so easy to lighten.

You will want a sharp point to color small areas with colored pencils so keep a pencil sharpener nearby. Any kind of pencil sharpener can be used. A small hand-held manual sharpener will give you the best control to smoothly sharpen your colored pencils to just the right point.

To remove a page for coloring, use a utility knife. Otherwise, if you are coloring with the pages in the book, place a protective layer of paper or cardstock behind your work to catch any color that bleeds through. To keep your borders free of overspill, low-tack artist tape can be used to mask off the edges.

Thank you so much for buying my book. Restoring these beautiful illustrations was truly a labor of love and I hope you enjoy coloring them. If you enjoy the book, please consider leaving a review at your online place of purchase to help others. ***New Testament Bible Story Illustrations*** and its companion book, ***Old Testament Bible Story Illustrations,*** are inspirational coloring books. They provide a perfect way to use your talents to make works of beauty and devotion. May you enjoy hours of calmness and contemplation as each page blossoms into your own unique creation.

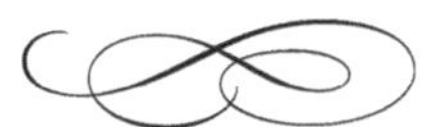

Each illustration is backed with its companion Bible story.

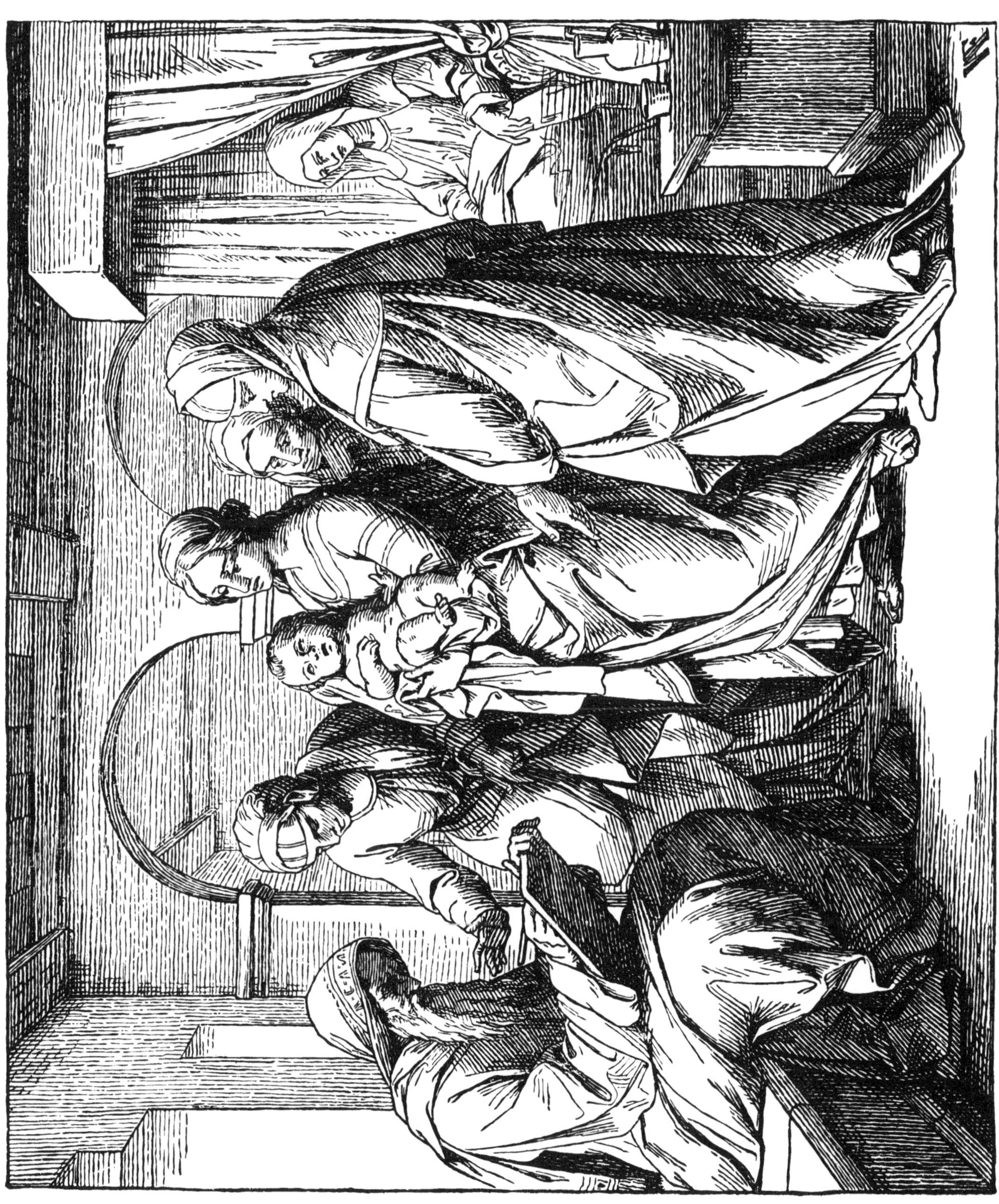

Zacharias Writing a Name for the Child

Zacharias was a priest at the time when people were expecting the Messiah to soon arrive. His wife was Elisabeth and they tried to please God in everything they did. But they were often sad that they never had any children. When it was the turn of Zacharias to go for a week to the temple to help in the services there, he prayed deeply and saw an angel of the Lord. The angel, Gabriel, had the good news that God was going first of all to send Zacharias and Elisabeth a son, and then — the Messiah was coming! The angel told Zacharias what his son's name was to be called, John.

The little Jew babies had a name given to them when they were eight days old. This baby's father, Zacharias, was dumb; he could not speak, but his friends said that his little child ought to be called Zacharias, like him. When his wife, Elisabeth, heard that, she said, Not so, but he shall be called John. And they said to her, There are none of thy relatives called by that name; and they made signs to Zacharias to know what name he would choose, for Zacharias was deaf as well as dumb, and he could not hear what they were talking about.

Then Zacharias asked for a tablet — a piece of wood covered over with wax, and he wrote on the wax with a pointed iron pencil. This is what he wrote, His name is John. The friends were surprised that Zacharias too had chosen that name. They did not know that God had told him to choose it.

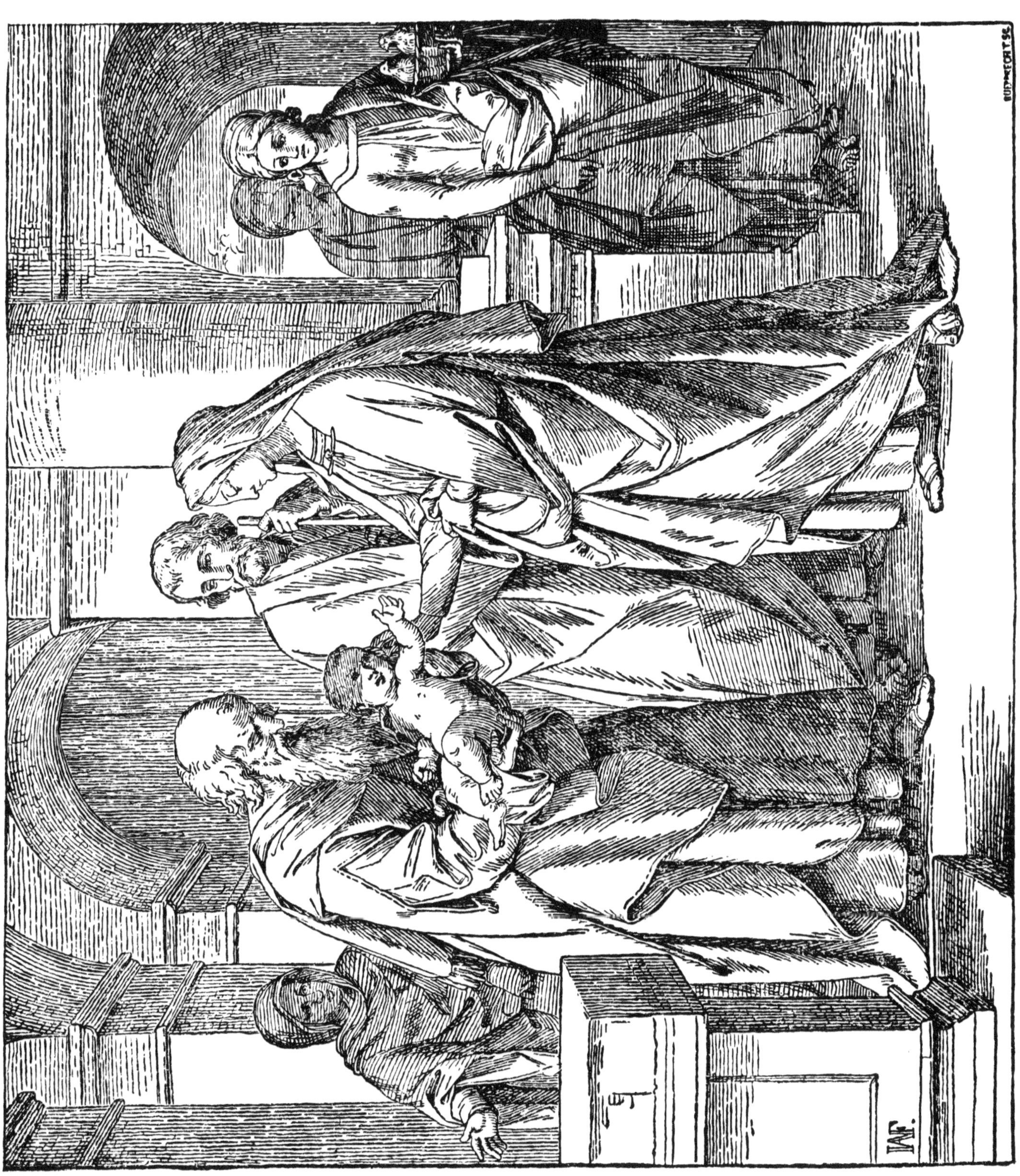

Simeon Taking the Child in His Arms

On the day when Jesus was presented to the Lord, the Spirit of God moved Simeon to enter the temple just at the moment when the priest had taken the child into his arms to bless him, and as soon as he saw the child, Simeon knew that this was he for whose coming he had been waiting so long. He took him up in his arms, and praised God, saying, Lord, now lettest thou thy servant depart in peace, according to thy word: for mine eyes have seen thy salvation, which thou hast prepared before the face of all people; a light to lighten the Gentiles, and the glory of thy people Israel. Joseph and Mary were filled with wonder at those things that Simeon had spoken concerning the child, and Simeon blessed them both, and told them again that this child would be the Saviour of his people.

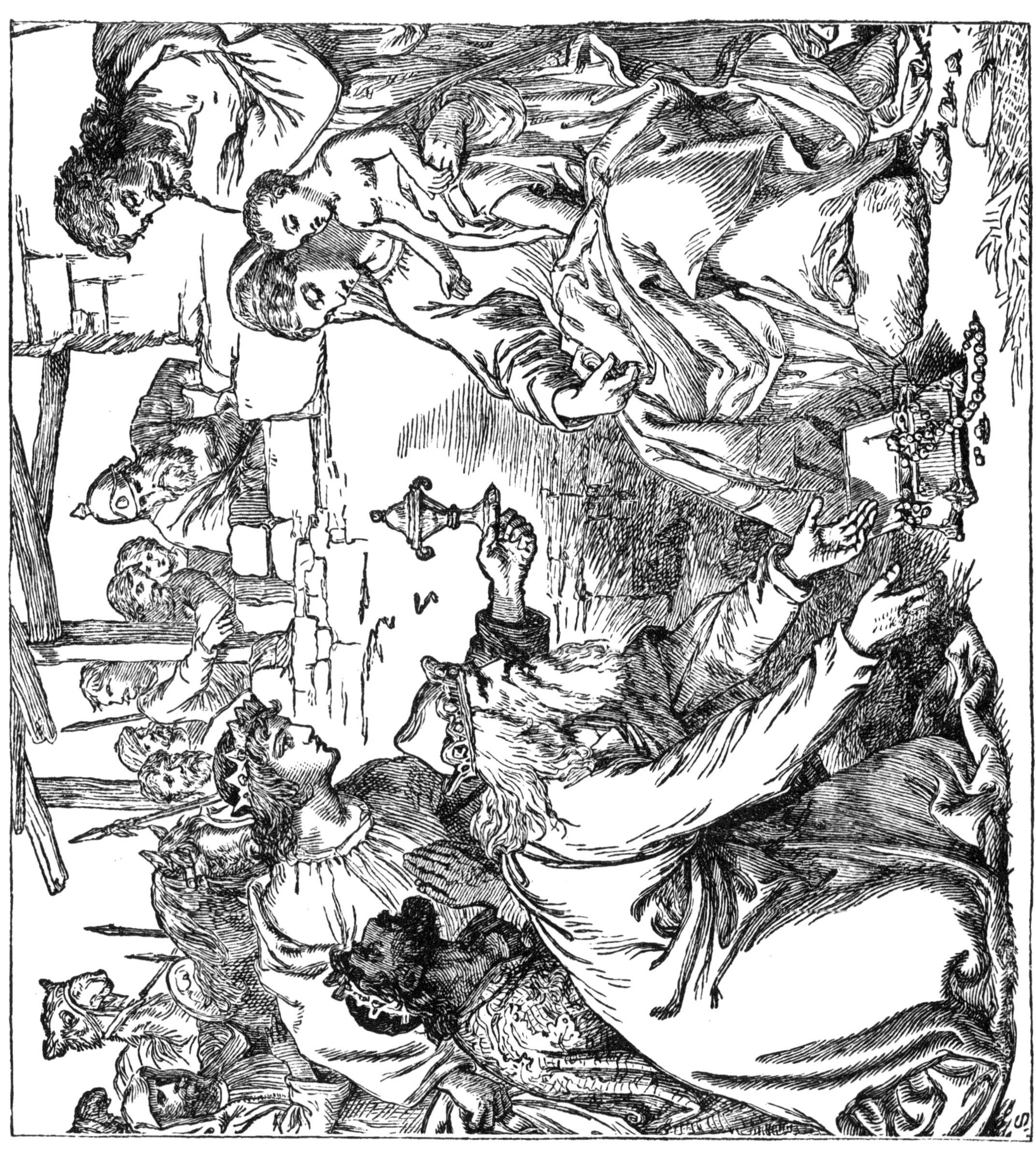

Wise Men of the East Presenting Their Gifts

The wise men journeyed to Bethlehem with their servants and their treasures, and the star went before them. When they reached the city, they inquired for the child that had been born of the kingly family of David, and were directed to the house where Joseph and Mary were now living. At last they had reached the end of their long journey, and now they were told that the King whom they had travelled so far to see was to be found, not in a palace, but in the house of a poor carpenter.

They made their way to the house that had been pointed out to them, and when they had come to it, they looked up and saw the star, which seemed to be shining right over it, and they rejoiced with exceeding great joy. Then they entered in, and found the young child and Mary his mother, and they fell down and worshipped him. And when they had opened their treasures, they presented unto him their gifts, gold and frankincense, and myrrh.

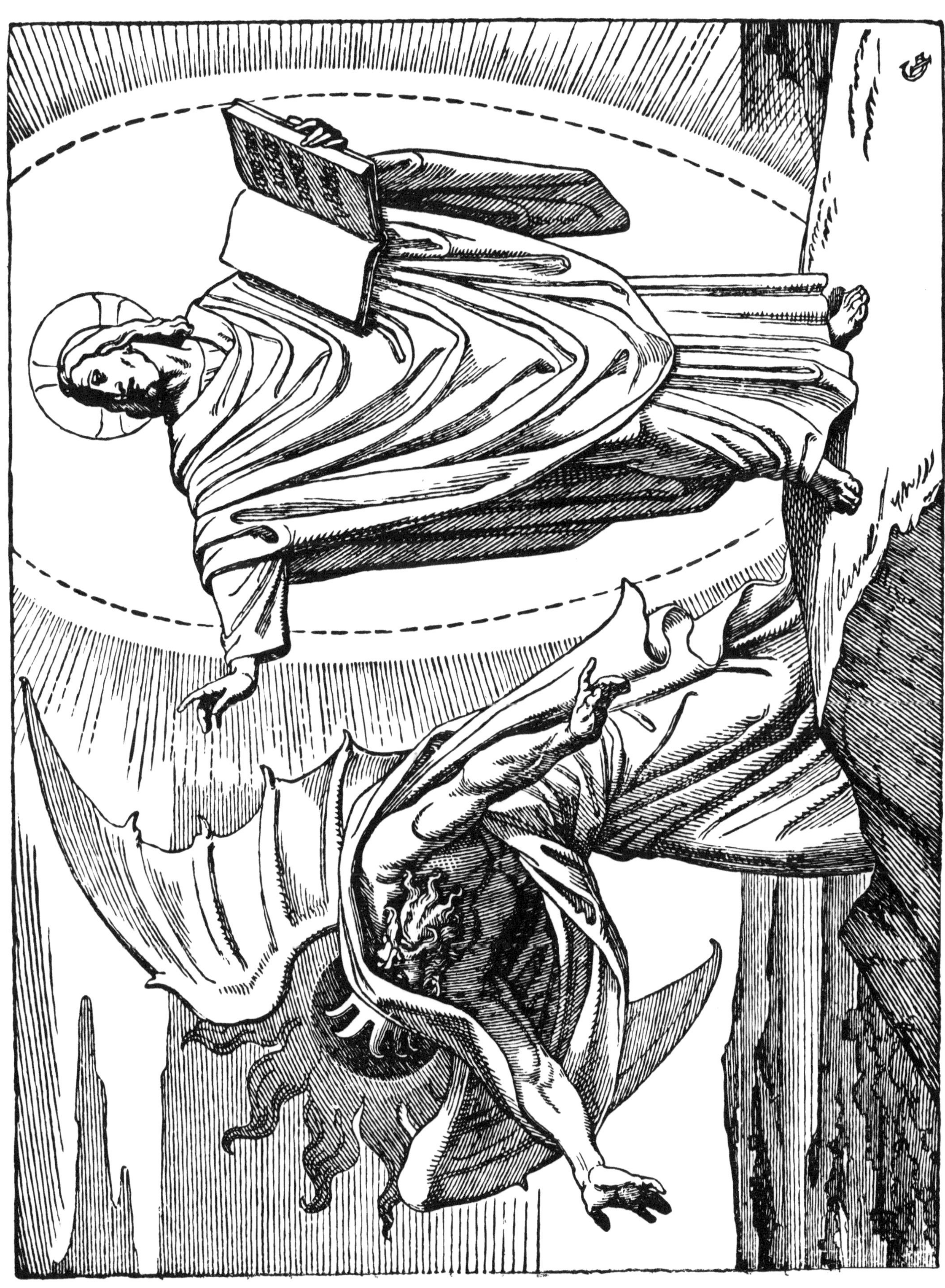

The Temptation on the Mountain

Satan took Jesus to the top of a very high mountain, and showed him all the kingdoms of the world, and all the beautiful things that are in them — all the thousands and thousands of people, all the gold, and all the treasures. Then he said to Jesus, I will give you all these things, and they shall be yours, if only you will fall down before me, and worship me. Jesus was very angry with the devil for daring to say such things. Go away, Satan! he said to him; for it is written, Thou shalt worship the Lord thy God, and him only shalt thou serve.

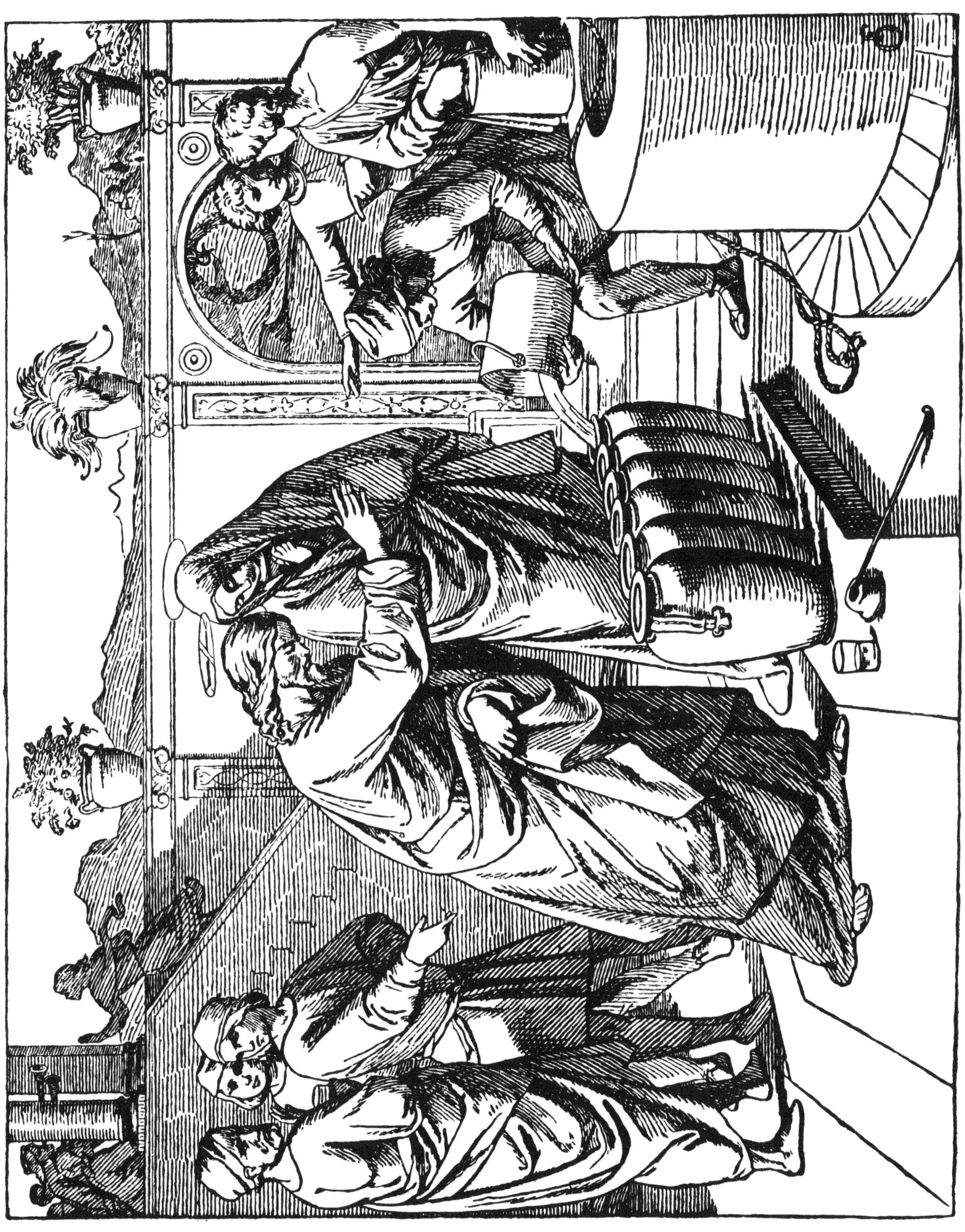

The Water Turned into Wine at Cana of Galilee

In a house a few miles away from Nazareth there was a wedding, and the mother of Jesus was there. Jesus was also invited to the marriage feast, and his disciples, and they went.

The people who gave the feast were poor, and they could not afford much wine; so after a little while it was all gone. The mother of Jesus knew that there was one sitting at the table who could help, and so she just simply said to her blessed Son, They have no wine. But Jesus answered her, What have I to do in this matter ? The proper time is not yet come for me to work. Jesus always waited for his Father's time, and not one moment before the right time would he do anything. He was as patient in waiting as he was patient in love and in suffering.

Mary felt quite sure that he was going to help them, so she turned to the servants, and said to them, Whatsoever he tells you to do, do it at once. There were some large stone jars in the room, used for holding water. Jesus said unto the servants, Fill those water pots with water. And they filled them to the very top. Then Jesus said, Now pour out some in a cup, and take it to the ruler of the feast.

The servants did as they were told; and when the ruler of the feast had tasted it he found that it was no longer water, but wine — the very best wine he had ever tasted. Jesus had changed into wine all the water that was in those large stone jars! So now there was enough, and more than enough, for all the guests.

The ruler of the feast could not understand where this wine had come from, so he asked the master of the house. But the master of the house did not know how it had come; he only knew that all he had was gone. But the servants knew all about it, and now they told the whole story: how Jesus had made them fill the great stone jars with water, and how he had turned all the water into wine.

The people were very much astonished at the wonderful thing their Lord had done; and it made them believe all the more firmly that he was the Son of God. And this is why Jesus did miracles; to show his power and glory, and to show people that he was the Christ.

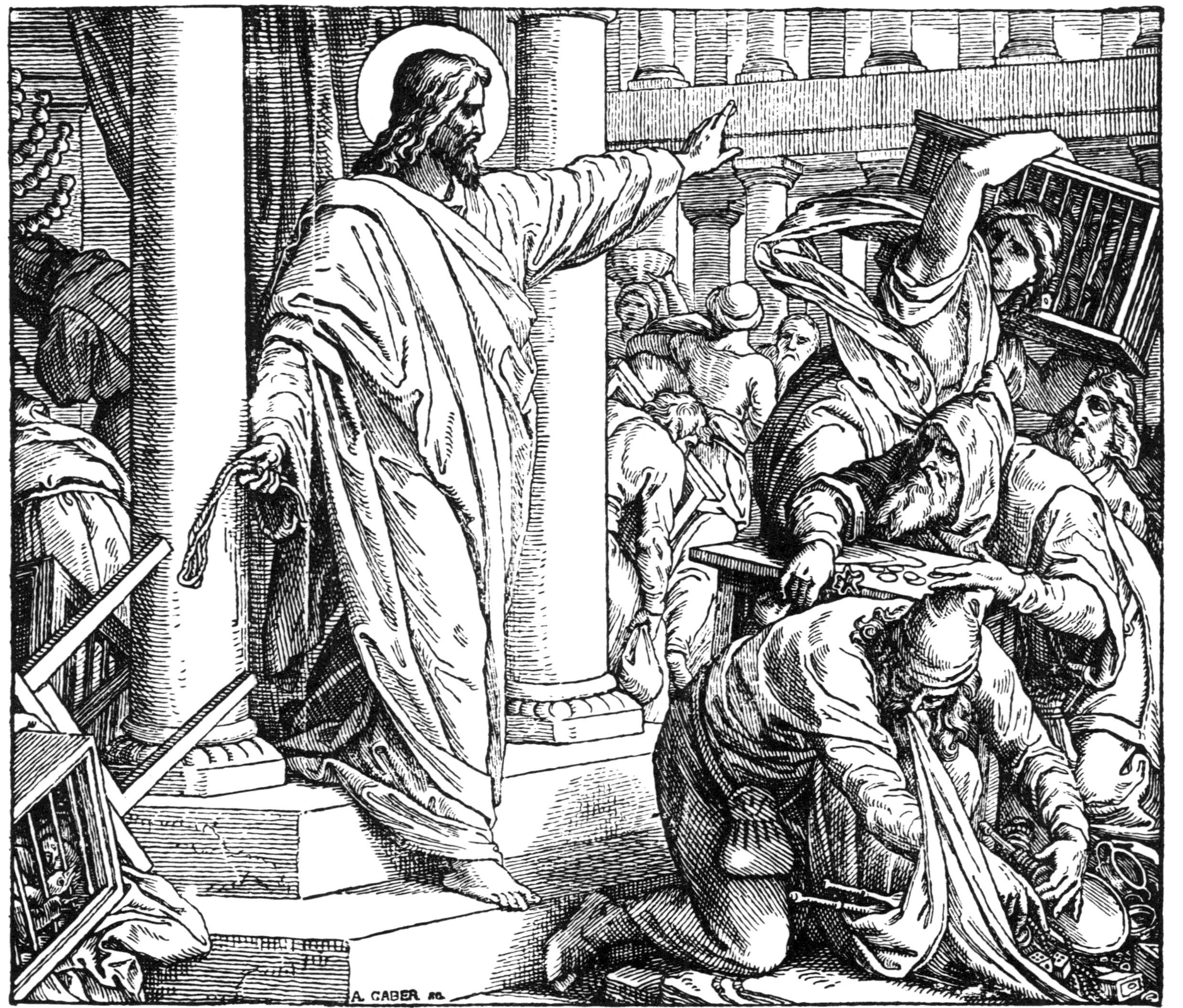
A. GABER sc.

The Money Changers Driven from the Temple

Very soon after his first miracle of turning water into wine, Jesus went to Jerusalem to keep the Passover. So Jesus went into the temple to join in the solemn services there, but what a sight met his eye! The grand entrance court of God's house was full of cattle, and crowded with men who were buying and selling them! Other men, with cages full of pigeons and doves, were offering them for sale! There were other men sitting before tables, on which were piled up heaps of money; these people were called money-changers. And all the noise of the men's voices, of the sheep bleating, and of the oxen lowing, could be heard in the inner part of the temple, where the services were going on.

Jesus was very angry at all he saw. He could not bear that his Father's house should be so dishonored; and in his holy anger he made a whip of small cords to chase out all those who were so profaning it. First he drove out all the sheep and the oxen, and those who were selling them. Next he went to where the money-changers were sitting, and he threw down all their tables, and upset the money that was piled up on each, leaving the men to grope about on the floor for all the coins which had been scattered. Then he said to those who sold the doves, Take these things away; do not make my Father's house a place for buying and selling. No one dared resist him. Though they hated him for what he had done, they felt in their hearts that he was right, and they were afraid of him. When the proud priests and Pharisees heard what Jesus had done, they did not dare complain; for they, too, knew quite well that they had done wickedly to allow such deeds to take place in the holy temple.

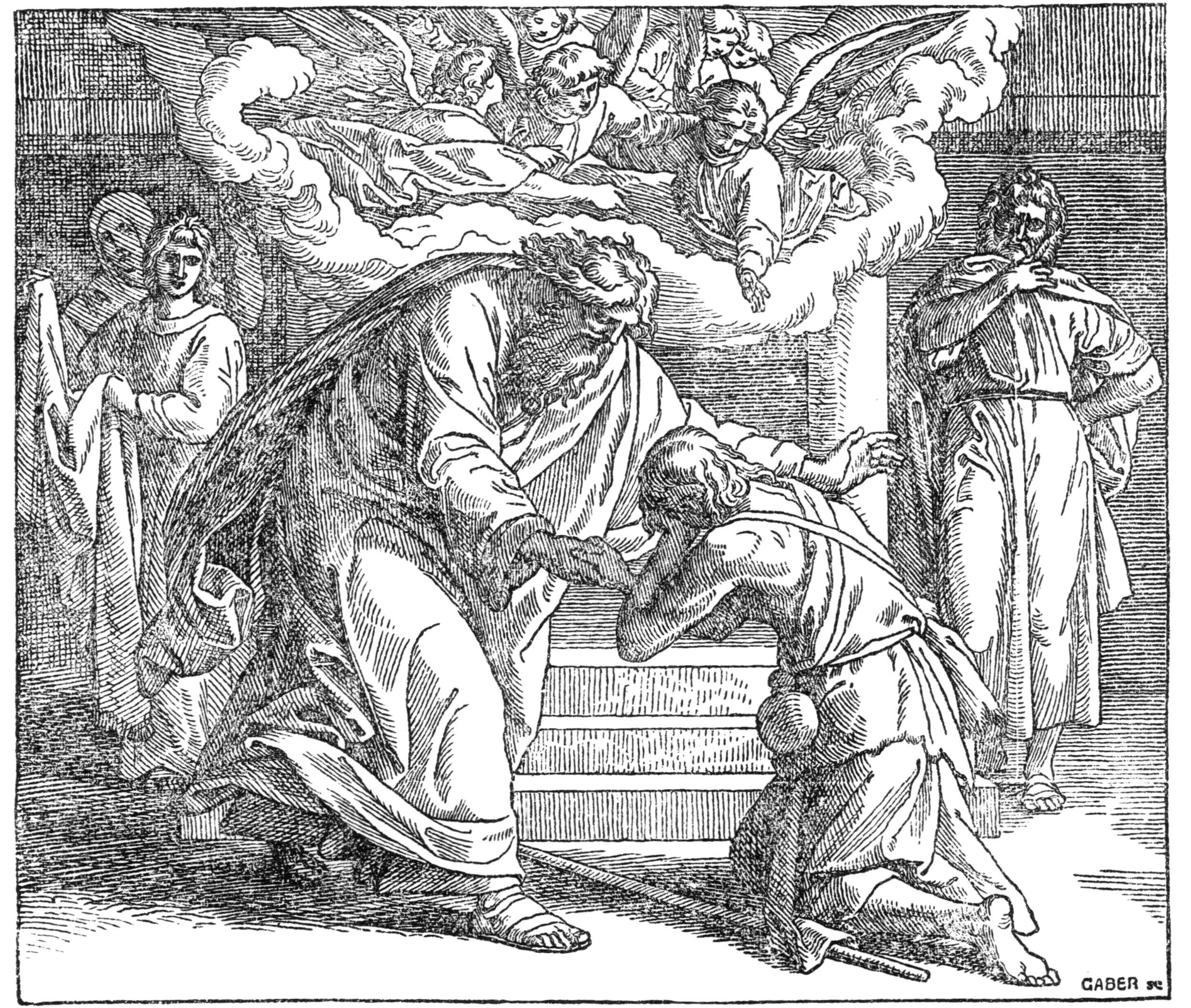
GABER sc

The Return of the Prodigal Son

Jesus told a parable of a certain man who had two sons. The younger son became tired of his home, and asked his father to give him the money that would come to him at his death, that he might go away and travel in foreign lands. The father yielded to his wishes, and the son went away to a far country, and had soon spent all the money in riotous living. When it was all gone, he began to be in want, for there was a famine in that land, and he became so poor that he was obliged to hire himself out as a swineherd. Even then he was often so hungry that he would gladly have eaten the swine's food, but no man gave unto him. Then he thought to himself, How many hired servants of my father have bread enough and to spare, and I perish with hunger. I will arise and go to my father.

This he did; and while he was yet a great way off, the father saw him, and had compassion, and ran, and fell on his neck and kissed him. And the son said, Father I have sinned against heaven and in thy sight, and am no more worthy to be called thy son. But the father said to his servants, Bring forth the best robe and put it on him and put a ring on his hand, and shoes on his feet, and bring hither the fatted calf and kill it, and let us eat and be merry. For this my son was dead, and is alive again; he was lost, and is found.

The publicans and sinners did not need to ask what the parable meant. They knew that the prodigal son represented such people as themselves, and that God was a kind father who was so willing to forgive his son as soon as he repented of his evil ways.

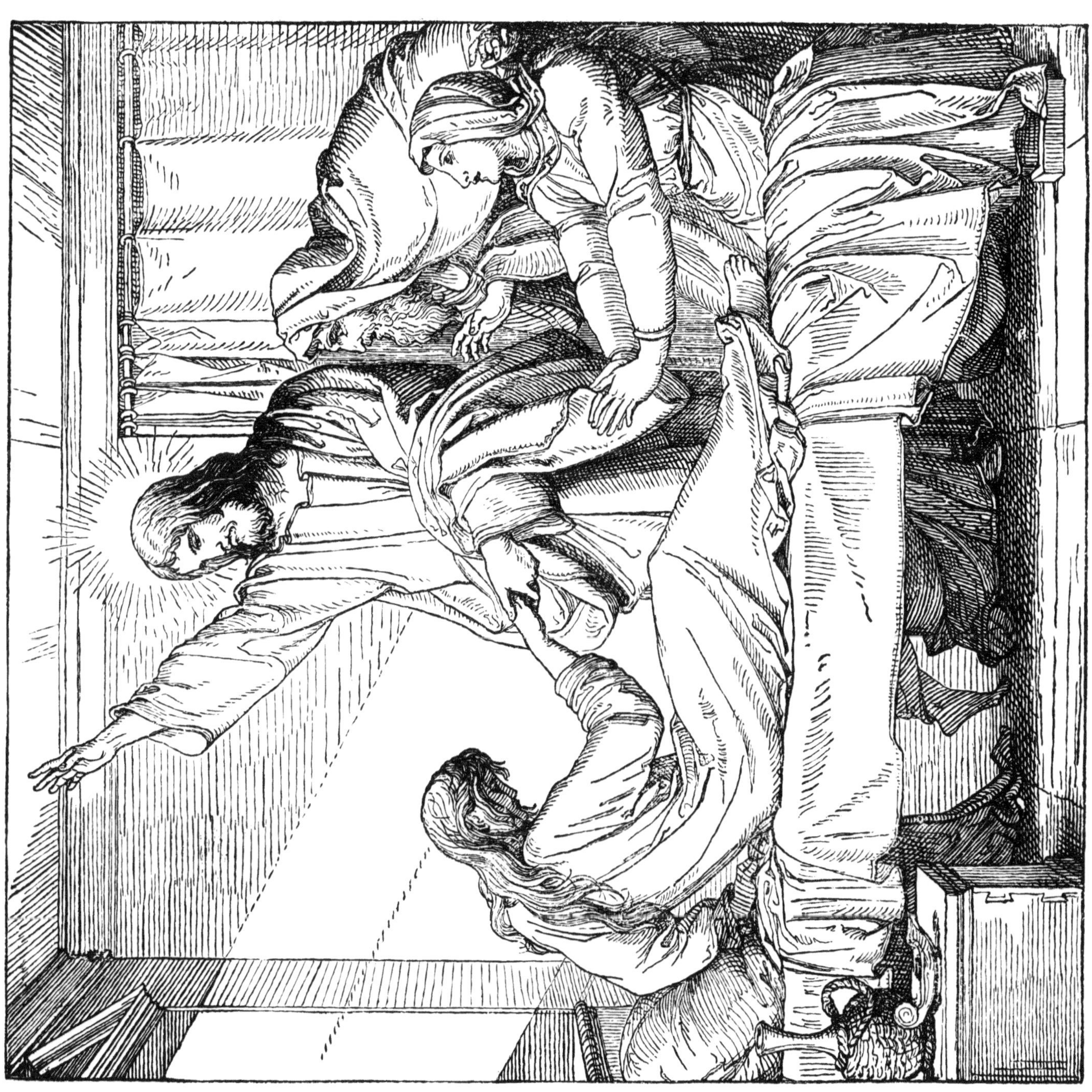

Christ Raising the Daughter of Jairus

There came to Jesus a man named Jairus, who was one of the rulers of the synagogue. He was running in great haste; and falling at the feet of Jesus, he besought him that he would help him, for he was in great trouble. My little daughter, he said, lieth at the point of death. I pray thee, come and lay thy hands upon her that she may be healed, and she shall live.

Jesus went with him and some messengers came from the house of Jairus, who said to him, Thy daughter is dead; trouble not the Master. But when Jesus heard it, he said, Fear not, believe only, and she shall be made whole. And he went with them towards the house. When they reached it, they heard a great sound of weeping and wailing; for it is the custom in the East, if anyone dies, to hire mourners to cry aloud and express the grief of the friends by many tears and lamentations.

Jesus would not allow anyone to enter the house with him, except the father of the child, and three of his disciples, Peter, and James, and John. Then Jesus went into the room in which lay the dead body of the maiden. All round her were the mourners, weeping and lamenting, but Jesus told them that there was no occasion for their sorrow, since he had promised to make her well. Give place, he said, for the maid is not dead but sleepeth.

They thought they knew better; they were sure that she was really dead, and they laughed him to scorn. But he put them all out of the room, and allowed no one to remain but the father and mother of the maiden. Then he went up to her, and took her by the hand, saying Hebrew words which mean, Little maid, I say unto thee, Arise. And her spirit came again, and she arose straightway, and he commanded that something should be given her to eat.

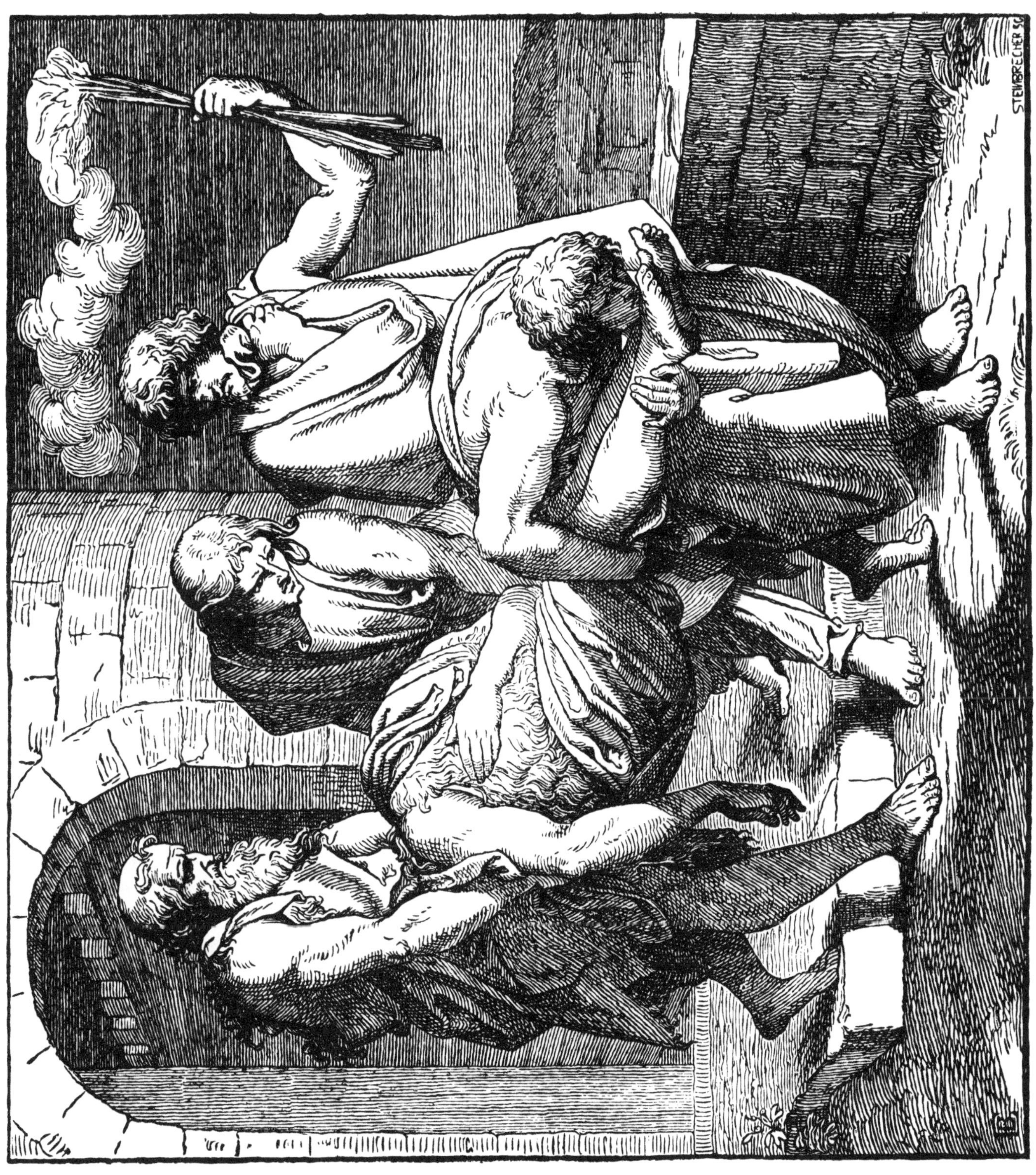

The Burial of John the Baptist

John the Baptist had an enemy in Queen Herodias. She was a very beautiful woman, who had been the wife of Herod's brother; but Herod had carried her off from his brother's house, and had married her himself. This was very wicked, and John said to Herod, It is not lawful for thee to have thy brother's wife. It was for this reason that the queen hated John. She would gladly have killed him if she could, but she had not been able as yet to accomplish her purpose, for Herod feared John, knowing he was a just man and holy, and he often sent for him, and heard him gladly.

But at last the opportunity came for which the queen had been waiting. It was the birthday of King Herod, and he had made a great supper for all his lords and high captains, and the chief men of Galilee. When the feast was ended, the daughter of Herodias came in and danced before them. She pleased Herod so well that he said he would give her whatever she should ask, and promised with an oath that she should have it, even if it were the half of his kingdom.

The girl went out and said to her mother, What shall I ask? And then the queen thought of her revenge, and told her to go back quickly and say, I will that thou give me here at once the head of John the Baptist in a dish. When the king heard what it was that the girl desired, he was exceeding sorry, but he had promised by an oath, in the presence of many witnesses, to give her whatsoever she should ask, and though he knew he should do a greater wrong by keeping his promise than by breaking it, he had not the courage to deny her.

He sent a messenger in all haste to the prison to command that John should be put to death immediately, and soon the bleeding head of the prophet was brought to him upon one of the golden dishes that had been used at the feast. He gave the ghastly present to the girl, and she took it and carried it to her mother. You may imagine how grieved and distressed the disciples of John were when they heard that the king had killed their dear master. They went to the prison, then lovingly and sadly took up the headless body, and laid it reverently in a tomb.

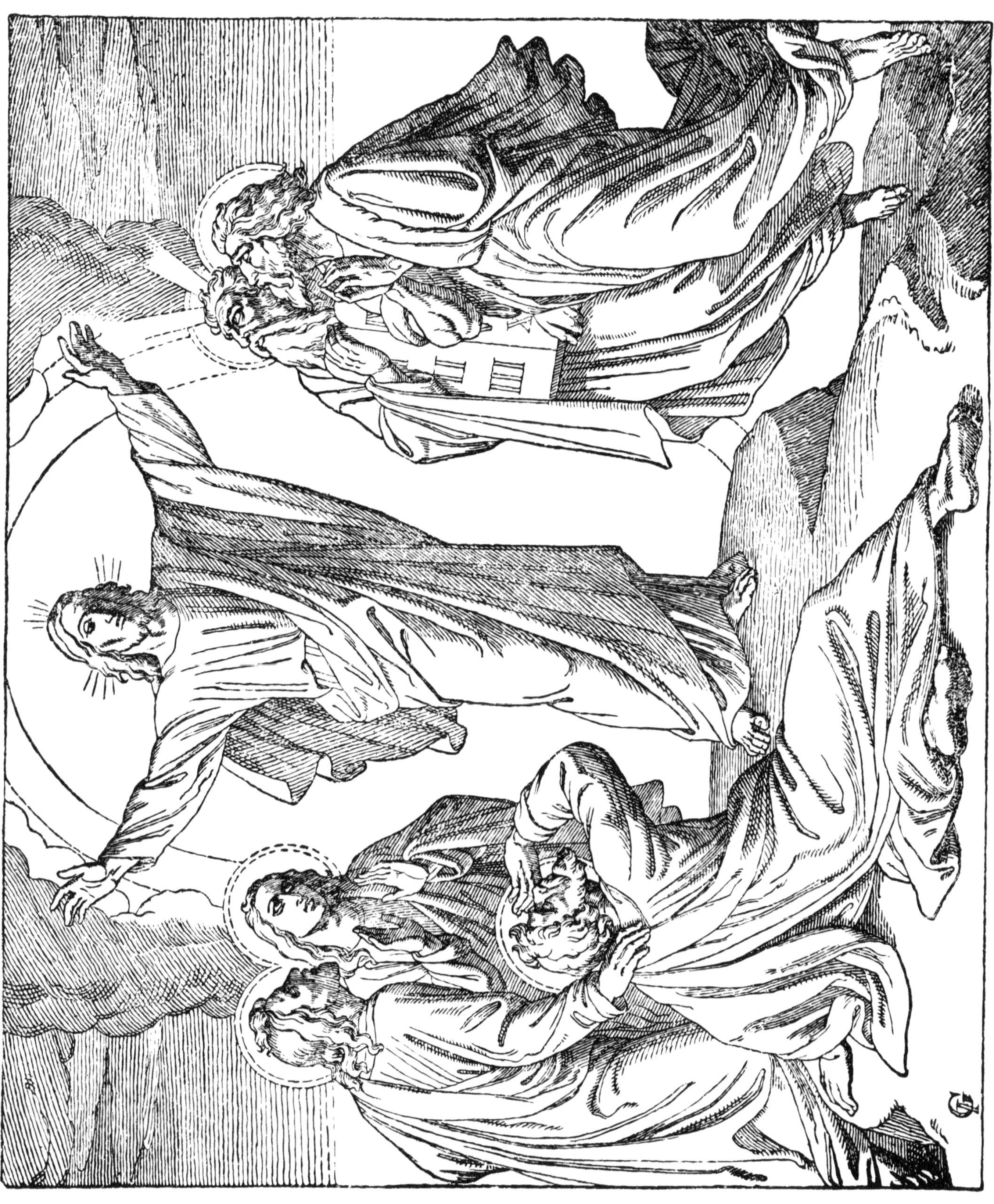

The Transfiguration

Jesus journeyed with his disciples to the summit of a noble mountain, covered with perpetual snow, called Mount Hermon. He went with the three disciples that he loved the best, Peter and James and John.

But after a time, the three disciples, who were tired after their day's journey, became heavy with sleep, and Jesus left them to lie down and rest, while he himself climbed, higher up the mountain, that he might spend the time in prayer. His mind was filled with the thought of all that was to befall him at Jerusalem, and he desired to gain strength from God to tread the thorny path that lay before him.

Meanwhile Peter and James and John had fallen into a deep sleep, but suddenly they awoke, and became aware that something very solemn and wonderful was taking place. Looking up towards that part of the mountain where Jesus had been praying, they beheld him transfigured before them. His countenance did shine as the sun, and his raiment was white as the light. And behold there were two others — Moses, the giver of the Law, and Elijah, the great prophet, who were talking with Jesus. They were speaking of his death, which was to take place at Jerusalem.

Never before had the disciples beheld so glorious a vision, and as they gazed upon the altered form of their Master, they were filled with awe and solemn rapture. They longed to continue looking forever on that wondrous sight, and Peter cried out, Lord, it is good for us to be here; and let us make three tabernacles, one for thee, and one for Moses, and one for Elijah. But even as he spoke, there came a cloud which overshadowed them, and the disciples feared as they entered into it. Then they heard a voice coming out of the cloud which said, This is my beloved Son, in whom I am well pleased. Hear ye him. And they fell upon their faces to the earth, overpowered with awe at the voice of God.

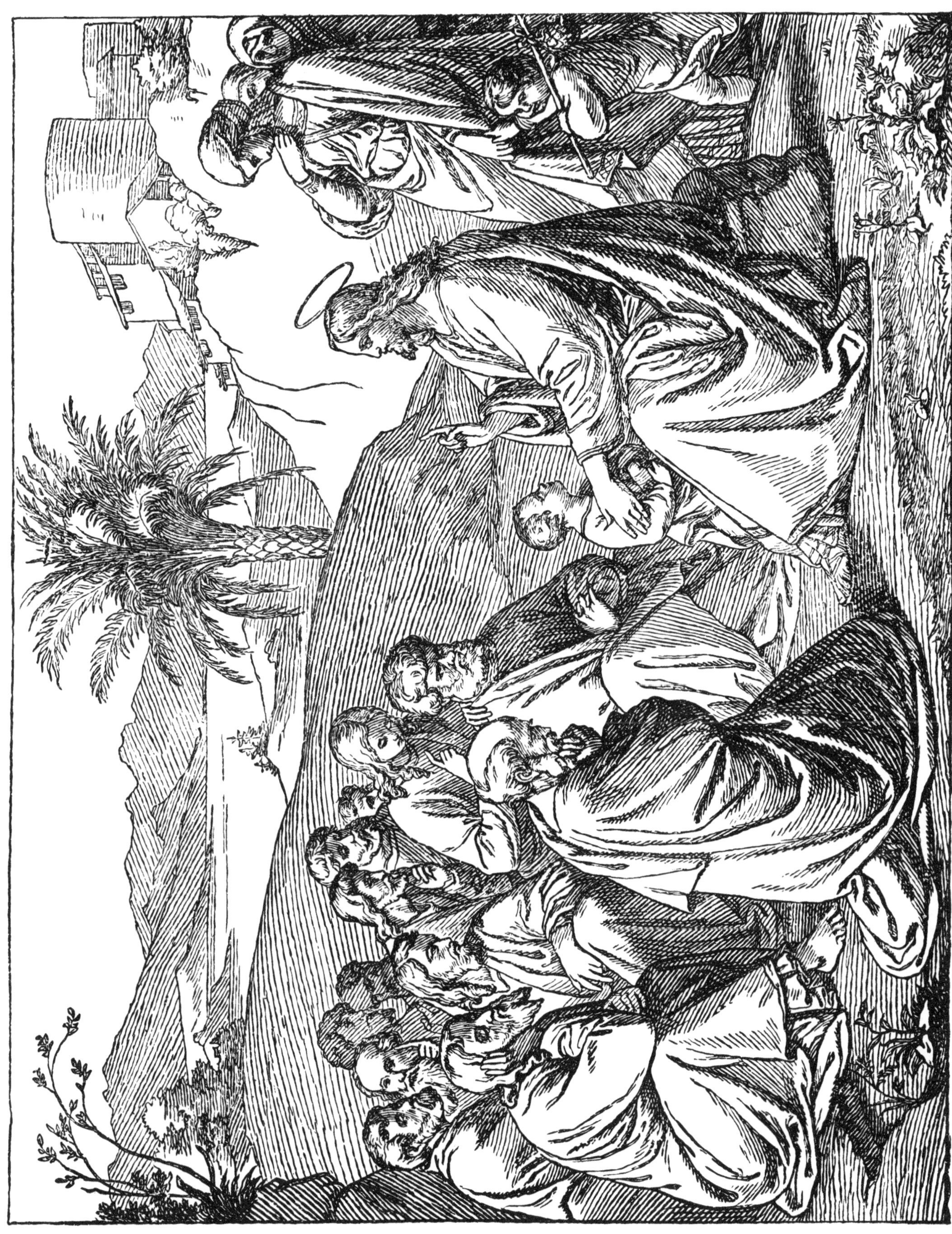

Jesus Teaching Humility by a Little Child

Jesus told his disciples that those who showed kindness to little children were really doing a service to himself, and that he would accept the kindness as if it were actually done unto him.

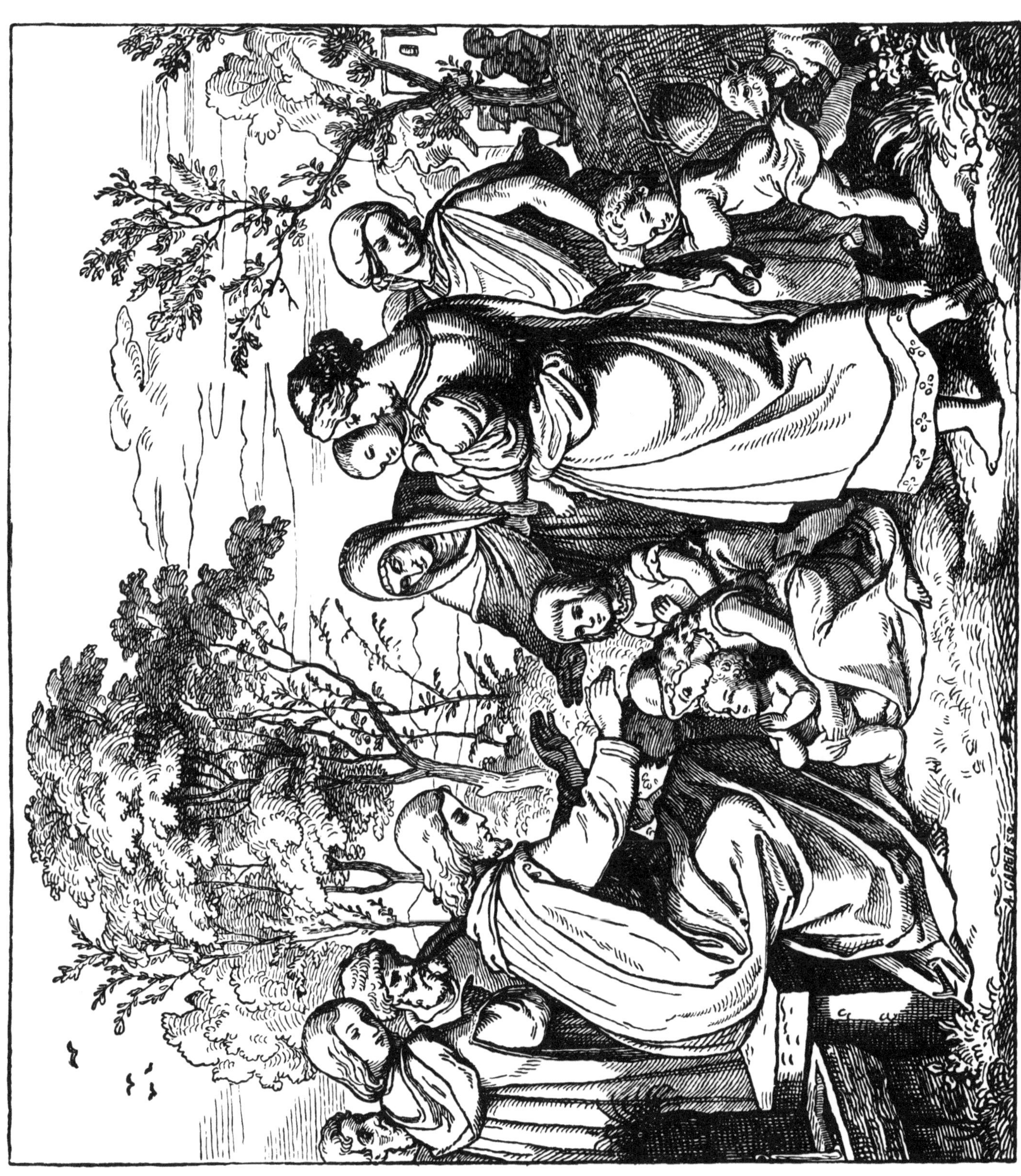

Jesus Blessing Little Children

One day, Jesus was about to enter a certain city towards evening, and the women of the place, who had heard of his coming from the messengers sent on in front, assembled together and brought out their young children that he should bless them.

Jesus was wearied with his journey, and when the disciples saw the crowd of women waiting for him, they rebuked them, and told them that they must not trouble the Master. But Jesus was angry with the disciples for wishing to send them away, and he said, Suffer the little children to come unto me, and forbid them not, for of such is the kingdom of God. Verily I say unto you, Whosoever shall not receive the kingdom of God as a little child, shall in no wise enter therein. And he took them up in his arms, laid his hands upon them, and blessed them.

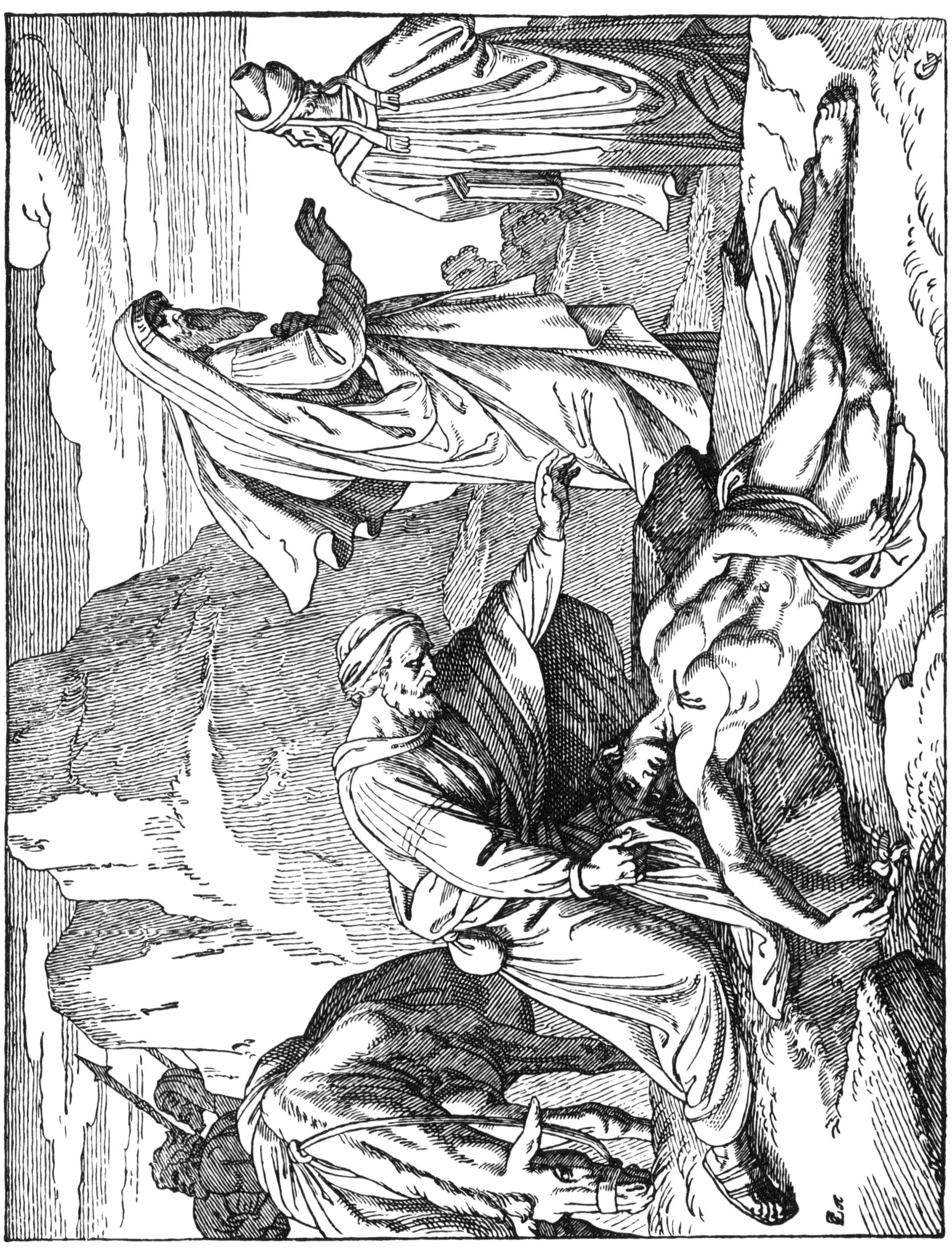

The Priest and Levite Passing By the Wounded Man

A certain man went down from Jerusalem to Jericho, and fell among thieves, who stripped him of his raiment, and wounded him, and departed, leaving him half dead. And by chance there came down a certain priest, but when he saw him, he passed by on the other side. And likewise a certain Levite, when he was at the place, came and looked at him, and passed by on the other side. After the priest and Levite passed by, a certain Samaritan, as he journeyed, came upon the wounded man, and when he saw him, he had compassion on him, and went to him.

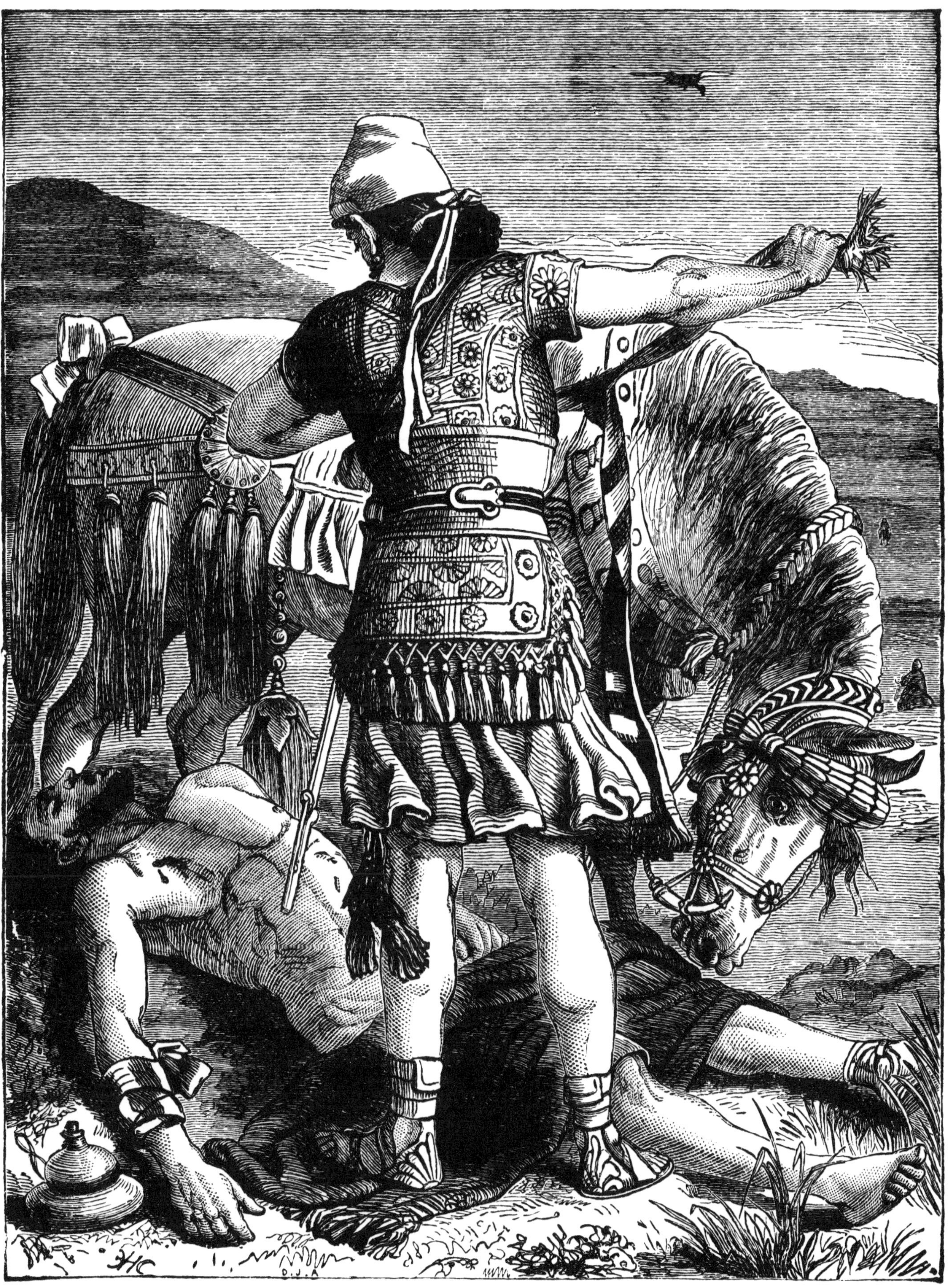

The Good Samaritan

The Samaritan bound up the wounds of the injured man, pouring in oil and wine, and set him on his own beast, and brought him to an inn and took care of him. And on the morrow, when he was departing from the inn, he took out two pence and gave them to the host, and said unto him, Take care of him, and whatsoever thou spendest more, when I come again I will repay thee. Now which of these three was neighbor to him that fell among the thieves? He that showed mercy on him. Jesus said, Go and do thou likewise.

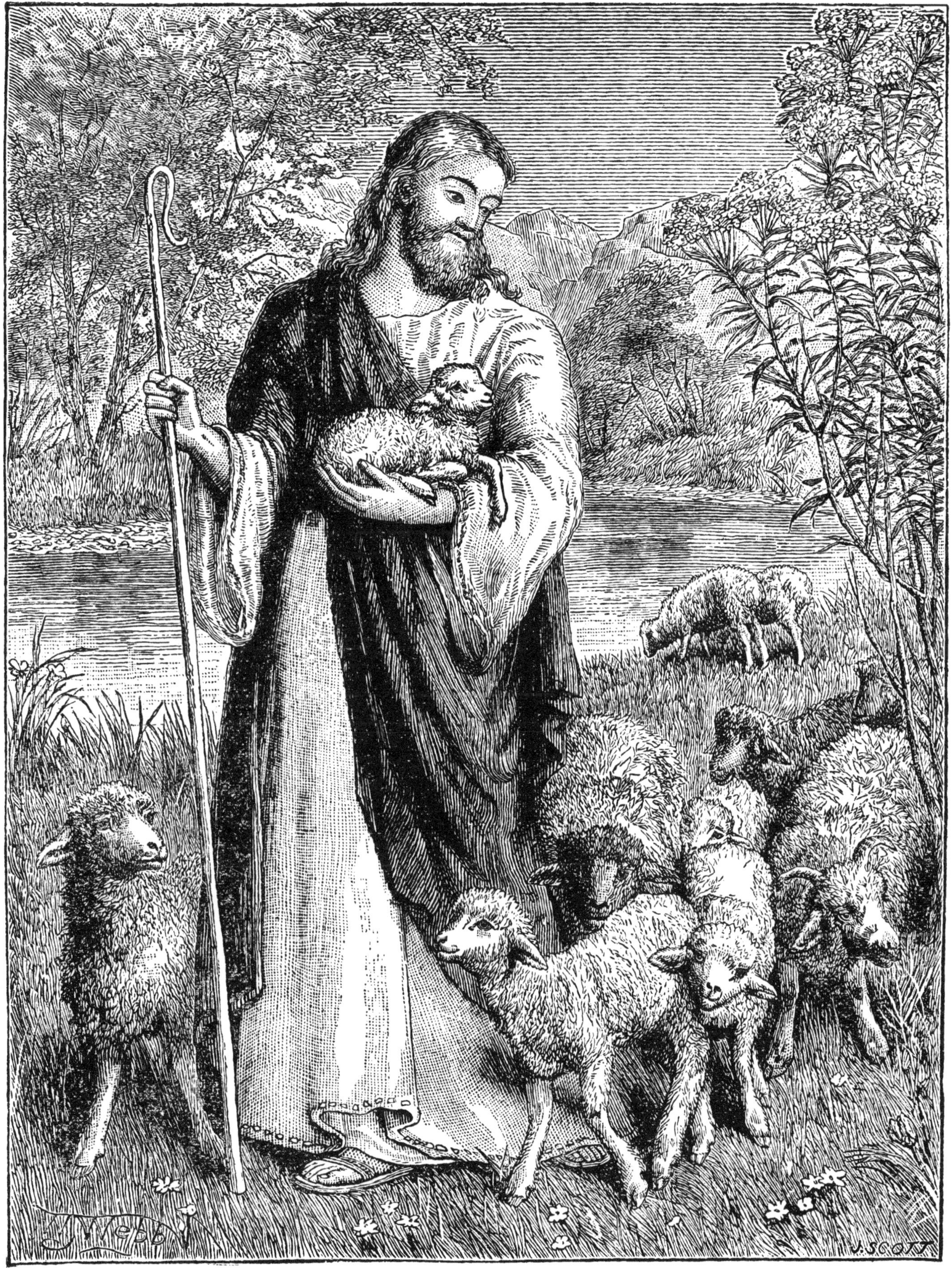
J Webb
J.SCOTT

The Good Shepherd

In one of his beautiful parables, Jesus compares himself to a shepherd: I am the Good Shepherd. The Good Shepherd giveth his life for the sheep. My sheep hear my voice, and I know them, and they follow me, and I give unto them eternal life, and they shall never perish and no one shall pluck them out of my hand. My Father who gave them to me is greater than all, and no man is able to pluck them out of my Father's hand. I and my Father are one.

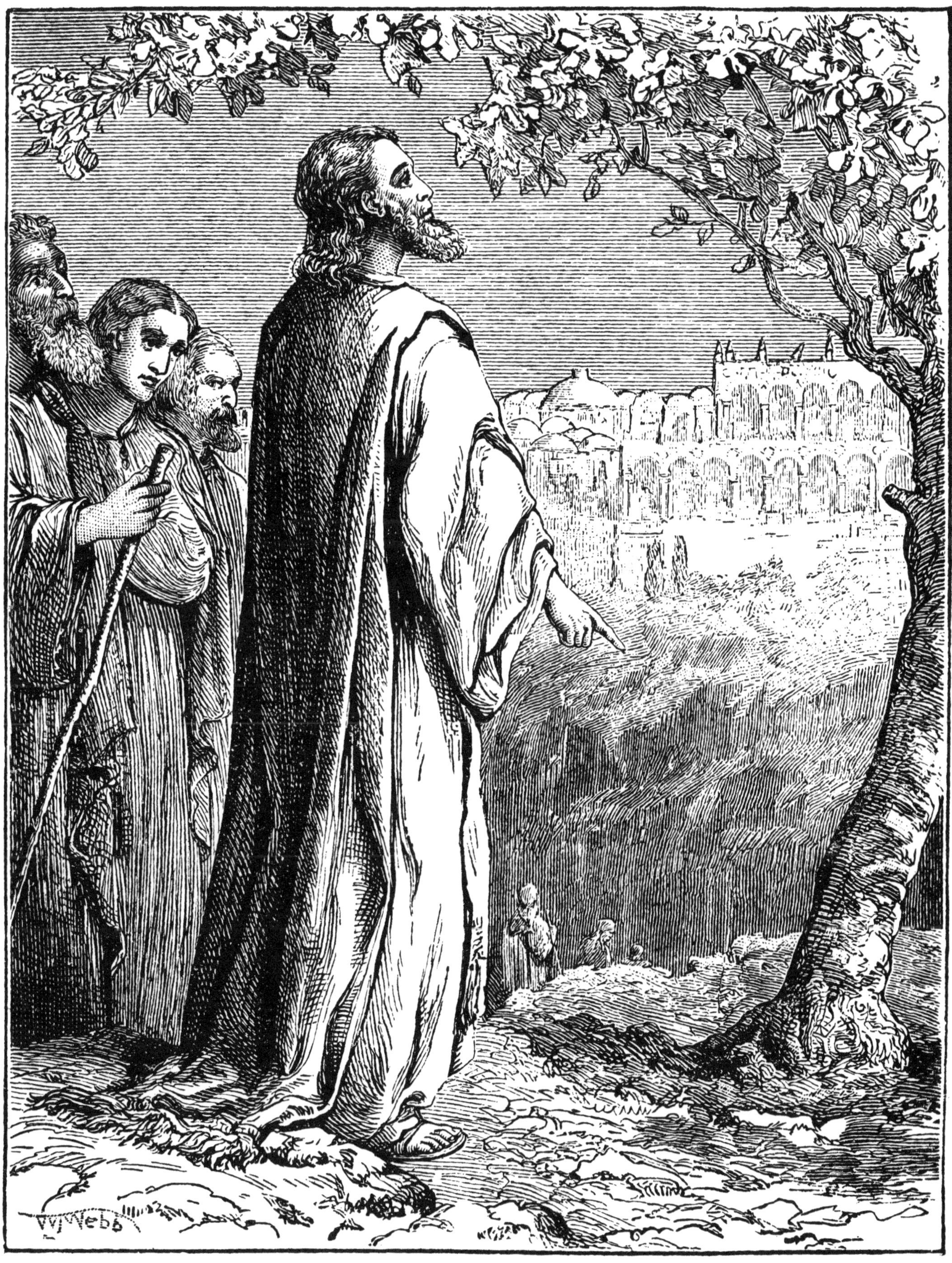
WJWebb

The Barren Fig Tree

One morning, when Jesus was coming towards Jerusalem, he was hungry. Seeing a fig tree afar off, covered with leaves, he came to it, hoping to find some fruit on it. But the tree was a young one, and had not yet commenced to bear fruit. And he found thereon nothing but leaves. Then he said unto it, Let no fruit grow on thee henceforward forever. And the fig tree withered away and was dead from the roots. When the disciples saw it, they marvelled, saying, How soon the fig tree is withered away!

Jesus answered, and said unto them: Verily I say unto you, if ye have faith and doubt not, ye shall not only do as I have done to this fig tree, but, also, if ye shall say unto this mountain, Be thou removed and be cast into the sea, it shall be done. And all things, whatsoever ye shall ask in prayer, believe that ye will receive them, and ye shall have them. And when ye are praying, forgive any that have injured you, that your Father also which is in heaven may forgive you your trespasses against Him. But if ye do not forgive, neither will your Father which is in heaven forgive your trespasses.

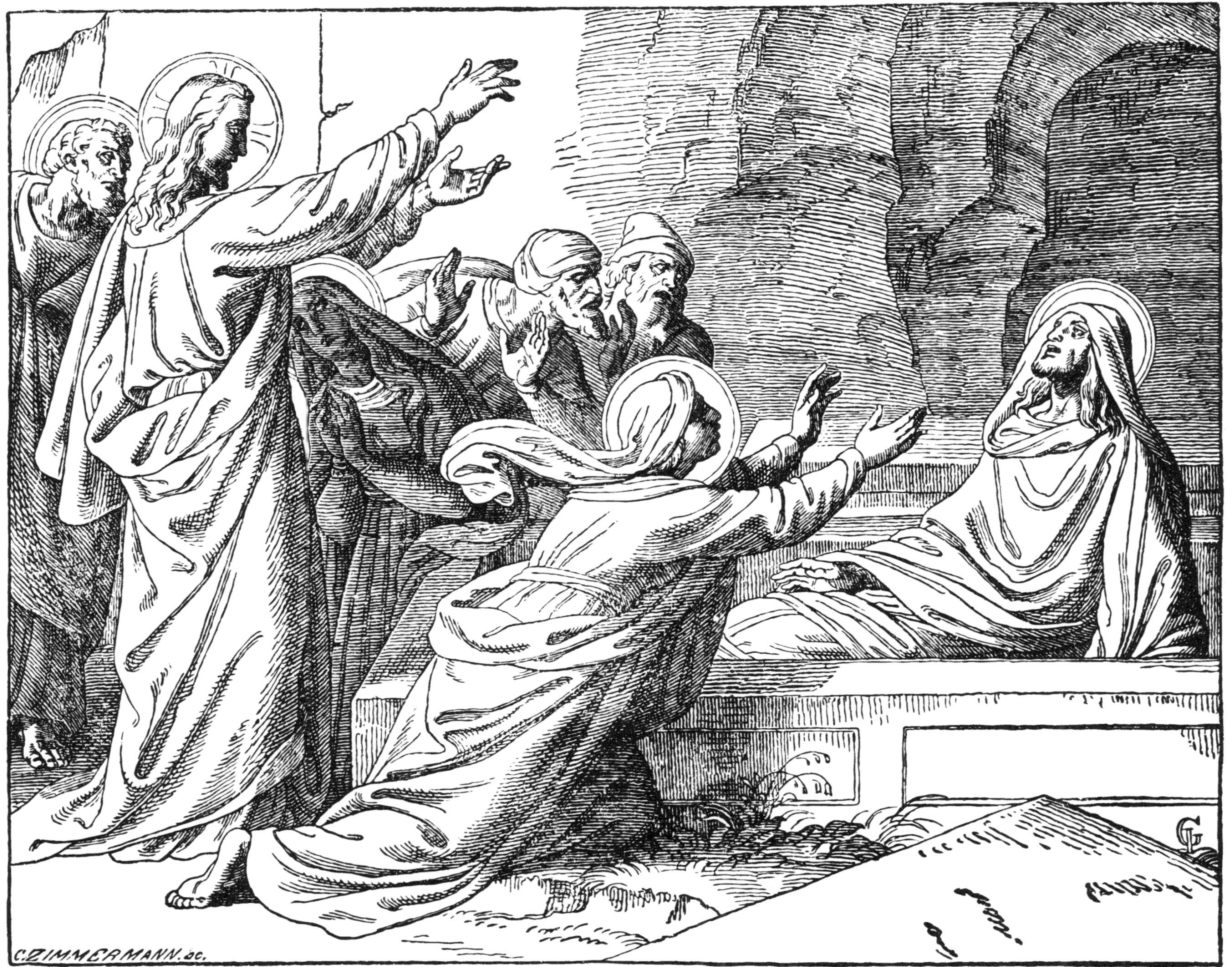
C.ZIMMERMANN.sc.

The Raising of Lazarus

Lazarus had been dead four days, and as is the custom in the East, he had been put into the grave on the very day of his death. Now Jesus loved Lazarus and his sisters Martha and Mary, and when he saw Mary weeping, and the Jews with her weeping also, he was overcome with anguish. Presently he said, Show me where ye have laid him. And when they had come to the grave, which was a recess hewn out of a rock, with a large stone slab in front to cover it, Jesus said, Take ye away the stone. When it was accomplished, Jesus lifted up his eyes to heaven, and said, Father I thank thee that thou heardest me. Then with a loud voice, he cried out, Lazarus, come forth!

As before in Galilee, so here in Judaea, that voice reached the ears of the dead man. Those who were standing round the grave saw a sight which to their dying day they never forgot. From out of the tomb, which for four days had been closed up, there came a figure, bound round and round with grave clothes, his feet and his hands tied together, and his face covered with a napkin. It was Lazarus, and Jesus told them to unfasten the grave clothes that he might move freely.

A great number of Jews had come to comfort Martha and Mary, but now there was no more need for consolation. The sorrow of the sisters had been turned into joy, their brother was restored to them alive and well, and the friends left them and went back to Jerusalem, many of them believing in Jesus.

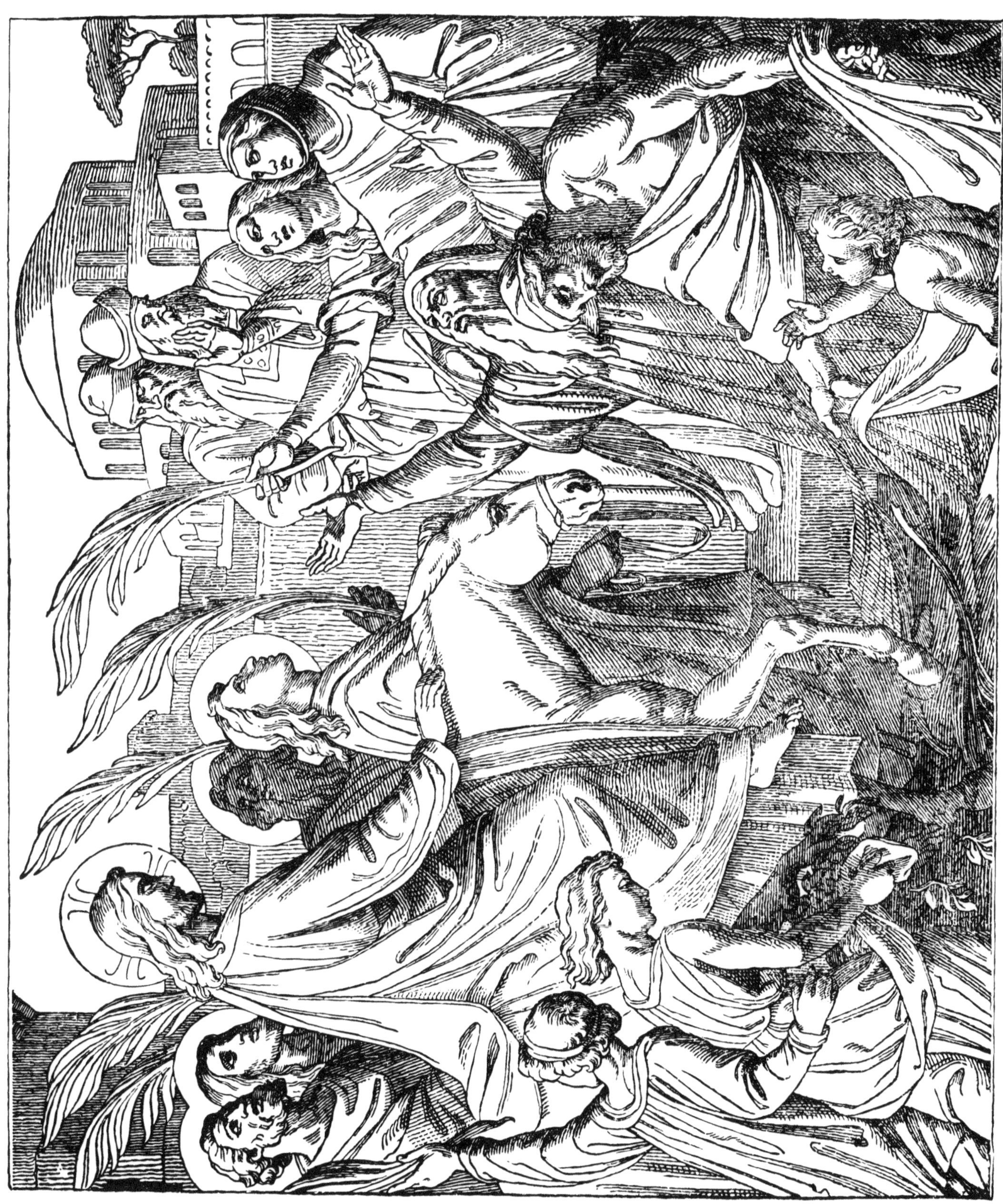

Christ's Entry into Jerusalem

On the first day of the week, answering to our Sunday, was the day on which at last the triumph of Jesus was to take place. He was to enter into Jerusalem accompanied by the multitude who had followed him from Galilee, and now, the disciples thought, the men of Jerusalem would surely be convinced, and be ready to acknowledge that Jesus was their long-expected Messiah.

Early in the morning, Jesus sent forward two of his disciples, and told them to go into the next village, where, he said, they would find a donkey and a colt tied together. These they were to unloose and bring to him, and if anyone saw them and asked them why they were doing this, they were to say, The Lord hath need of them.

The disciples did as they were commanded and brought back the donkey and colt, that Jesus might ride in state into the city. It had been the custom in the East for kings and great men to ride upon donkeys on grand occasions, and the disciples remembered how one of the old prophets had written, Rejoice greatly, O daughter of Zion, shout, O daughter of Jerusalem; behold, thy King cometh unto thee; he is just, and having salvation; lowly, and riding upon a donkey, and upon a colt.

The followers of Jesus had come out from the city to meet him, and when they saw him riding towards them on the colt, they shouted aloud for joy, saying, Hosanna to the Son of David! Blessed is he that cometh in the name of the Lord! Hosanna in the highest!

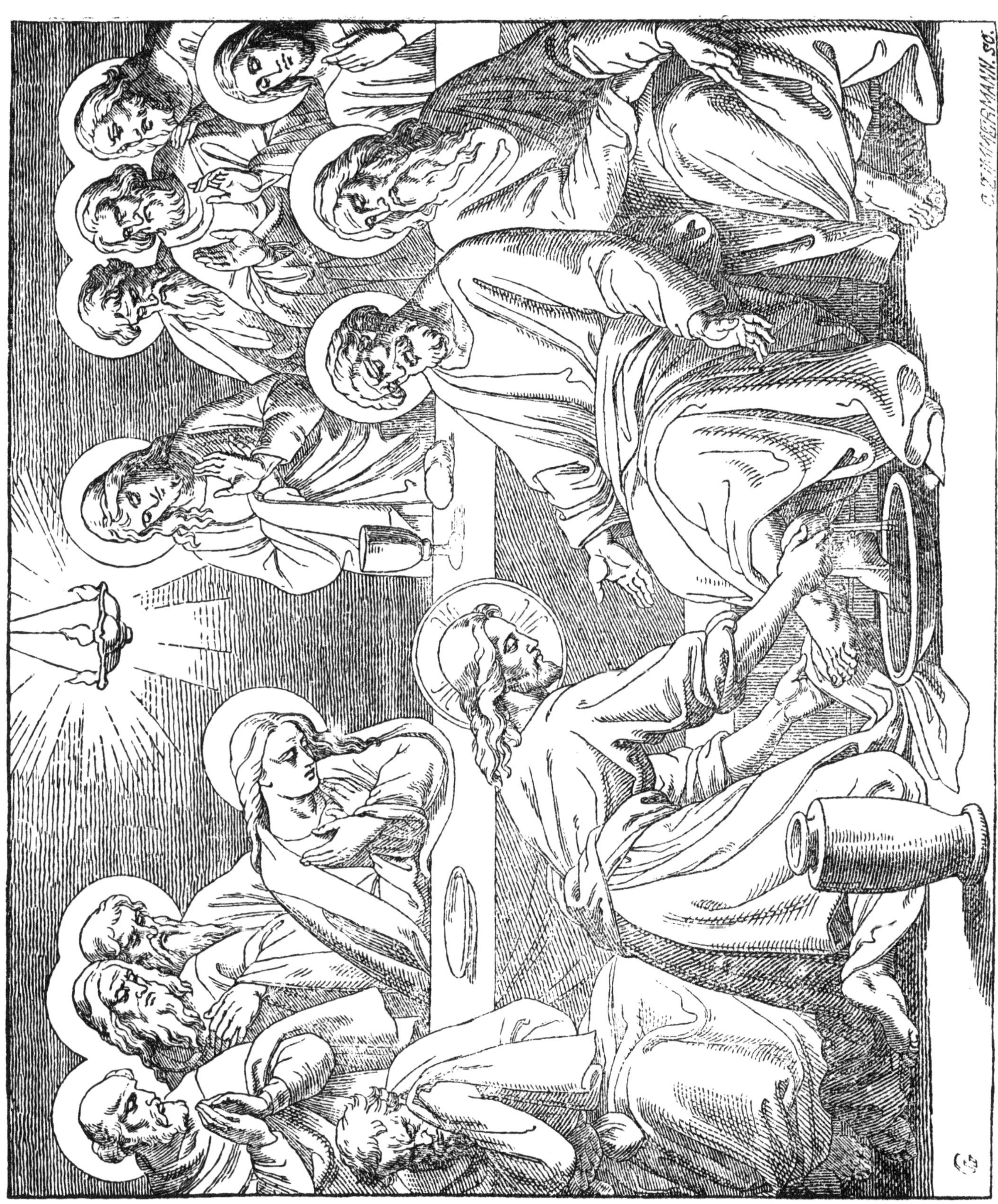

Jesus Washing the Feet of His Disciples

In the evening, when it was dark, Jesus came to the house where he was to eat at the Passover with his disciples; and there, in an upper chamber, they ate together the solemn meal.

It was the custom among the Jews to take off their shoes on entering a room, and to wash their feet and hands before eating, but on this occasion the washing had been left undone, for the disciples had been occupied in disputing as to which of them was the greatest and had a right to the most honorable place, and none of them had cared to render this service to the rest. Jesus therefore determined to teach them by his action that which was the lesson of his whole life, namely, that the greatest of all, is he who most truly serves his fellowmen.

He himself, though he knew that the Father had given all things into his hands, and that he had come from God and was going to God, rose from supper, and laid aside his upper garment, and took a towel and wound it round him. After that, he poured water into a basin, and, going to the disciples, one by one, he began to wash their feet, and to wipe them with the towel that was round him.

This was usually the work of the humblest slave, and when Jesus came to Simon Peter, the disciple could not bear that his Master should render him this service. He said, Lord, dost thou wash my feet? Thou shalt never wash my feet. But Jesus told him that it was his will to do so, and then Peter yielded.

When the feet of all had been washed, Jesus put on his garment and sat down again, and then he explained to them the meaning of what he had done. He said to them, Know ye what I have done unto you? Ye call me Master and Lord, and ye say well, for so I am. If I then, your Lord and Master, have washed your feet, ye also ought to wash one another's feet. For I have given an example, that ye should do as I have done unto you. A new commandment I give unto you, that ye love one another; as I have loved you, that ye also love one another. By this shall all men know that ye are my disciples, if ye have love one to another.

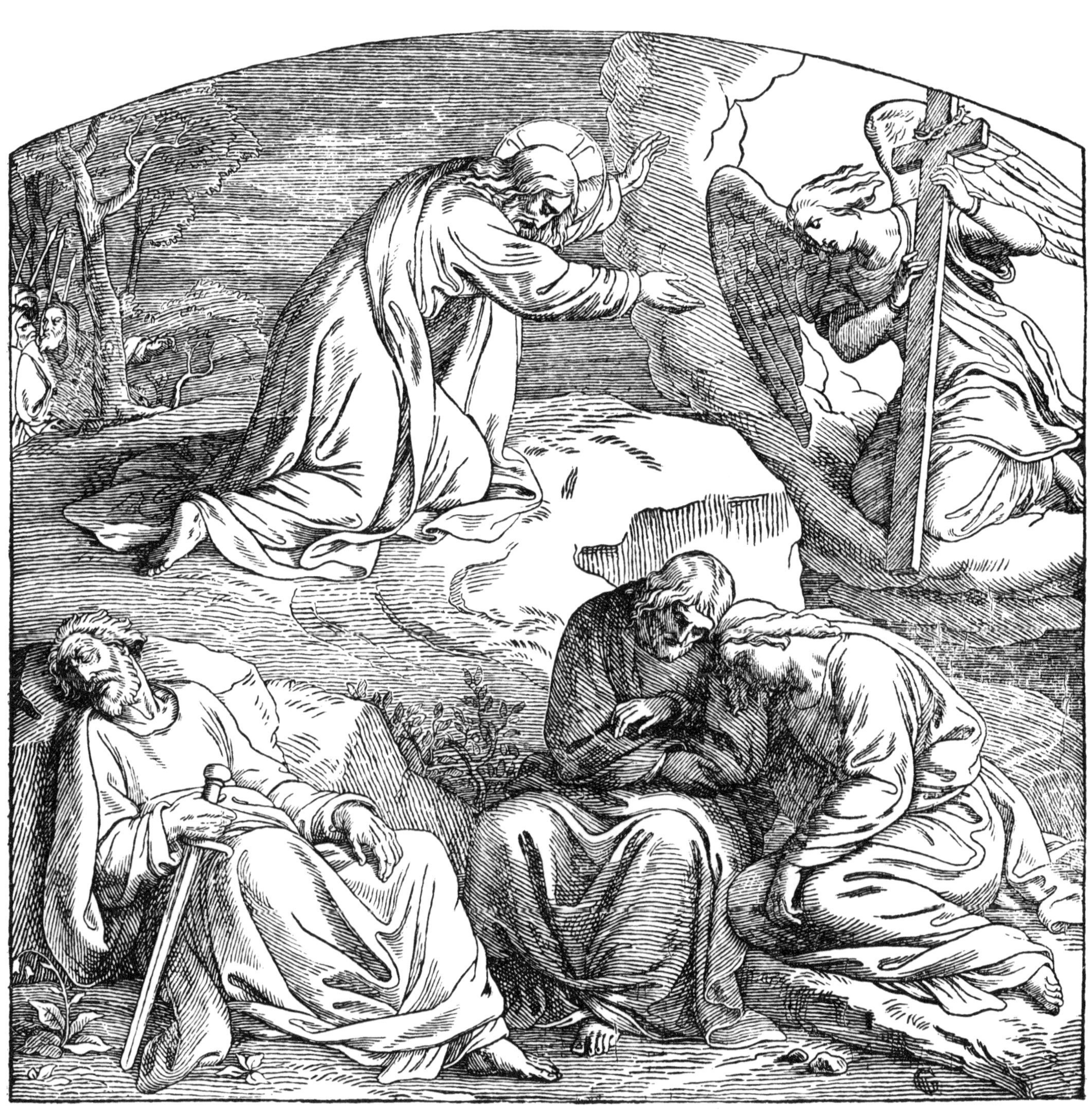

Christ in the Garden of Gethsemane

On the Mount of Olives there was a garden, called the Garden of Gethsemane, to which Jesus often went with his disciples. It was to this place that he now led them, and as they were going, he began to tell them how, that night, the Shepherd would be smitten, and the sheep of his flock would be scattered abroad. He was going to be betrayed, he said, into the hands of wicked men, and his disciples would all forsake him and flee away.

Peter could not believe that he should forsake his Master in the hour of danger, and he said, Though all should be offended because of thee, yet will not I. I am ready to follow thee both to prison and to death. But Jesus answered, I tell thee, Peter, that the cock shall not crow, until thou hast thrice denied that thou knowest me.

When they had come to the garden, Jesus left the rest of the disciples at a certain place, saying to them, Sit ye here while I go and pray yonder, and went on, with only the three that he loved the most, Peter and James and John. They were the three who had gone with him to pray on Mount Hermon, when he was transfigured before them; and now that his soul was troubled, he again desired that they only should be with him.

He said to them, My soul is exceeding sorrowful, even unto death; tarry ye here and watch with me. Then he went a little farther, and fell on his face and prayed, saying, O my Father, if it be possible, let this cup pass from me; nevertheless, not as I will, but as thou wilt.

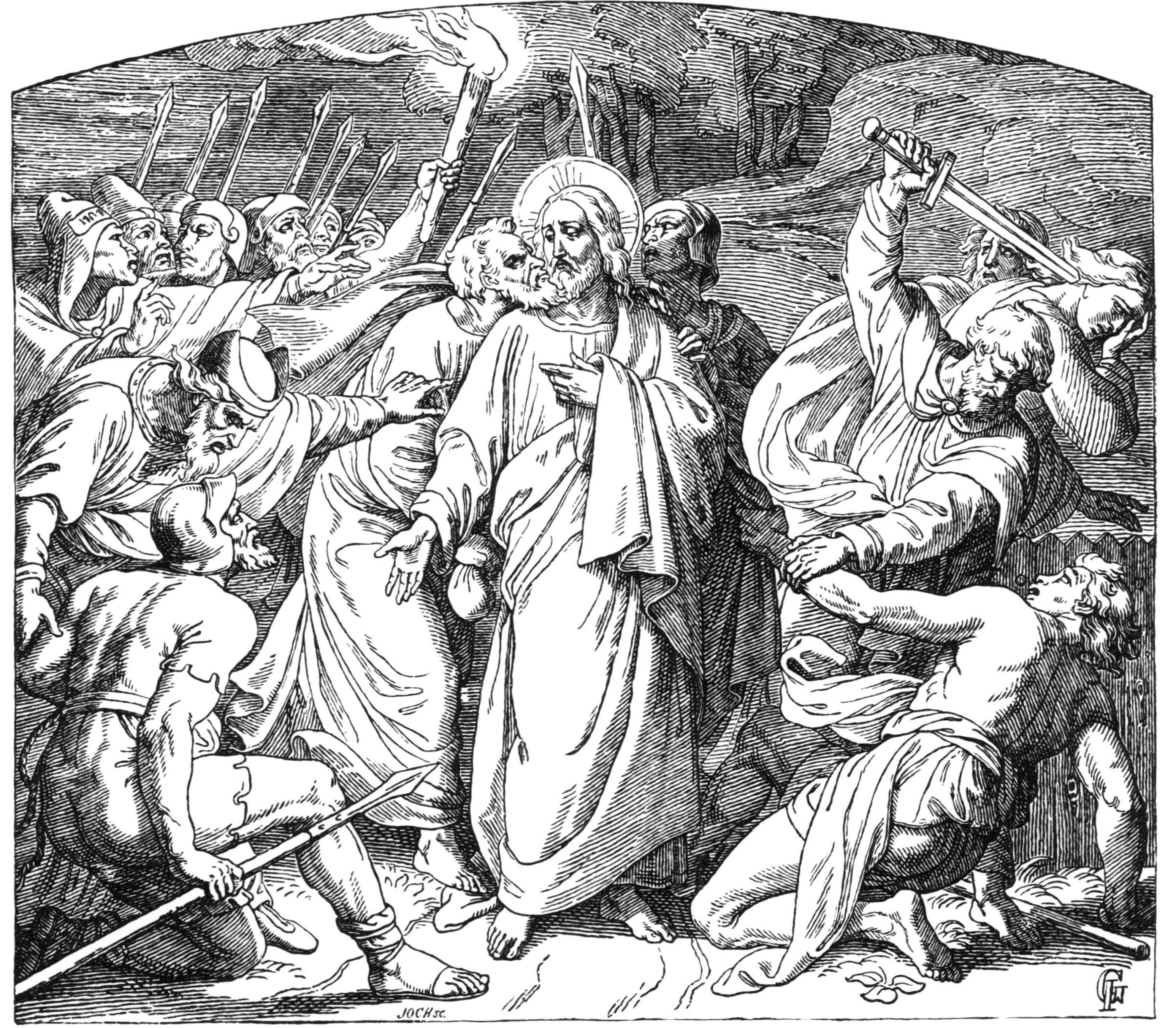
JOCH sc.

Judas Betraying Jesus with a Kiss

An armed band approached the Garden of Gethsemane, some of the men being servants of the High Priest, and others, Roman soldiers who were acting under his orders. At their head was Judas, who went before to show them the way. He had given a sign to the soldiers, saying, Whomsoever I shall kiss, that is he; take him, and lead him away safely. When they reached the place, he hurried forward, and going up to Jesus, he said, Hail Master, and kissed him.

But Jesus said, Judas, betrayest thou the Son of Man with a kiss? Then he turned toward the soldiers, and asked them. Whom seek ye? They said, Jesus of Nazareth. He answered, I am he; and as he spoke these words, they staggered backwards and fell to the ground, overawed by the majesty of his presence.

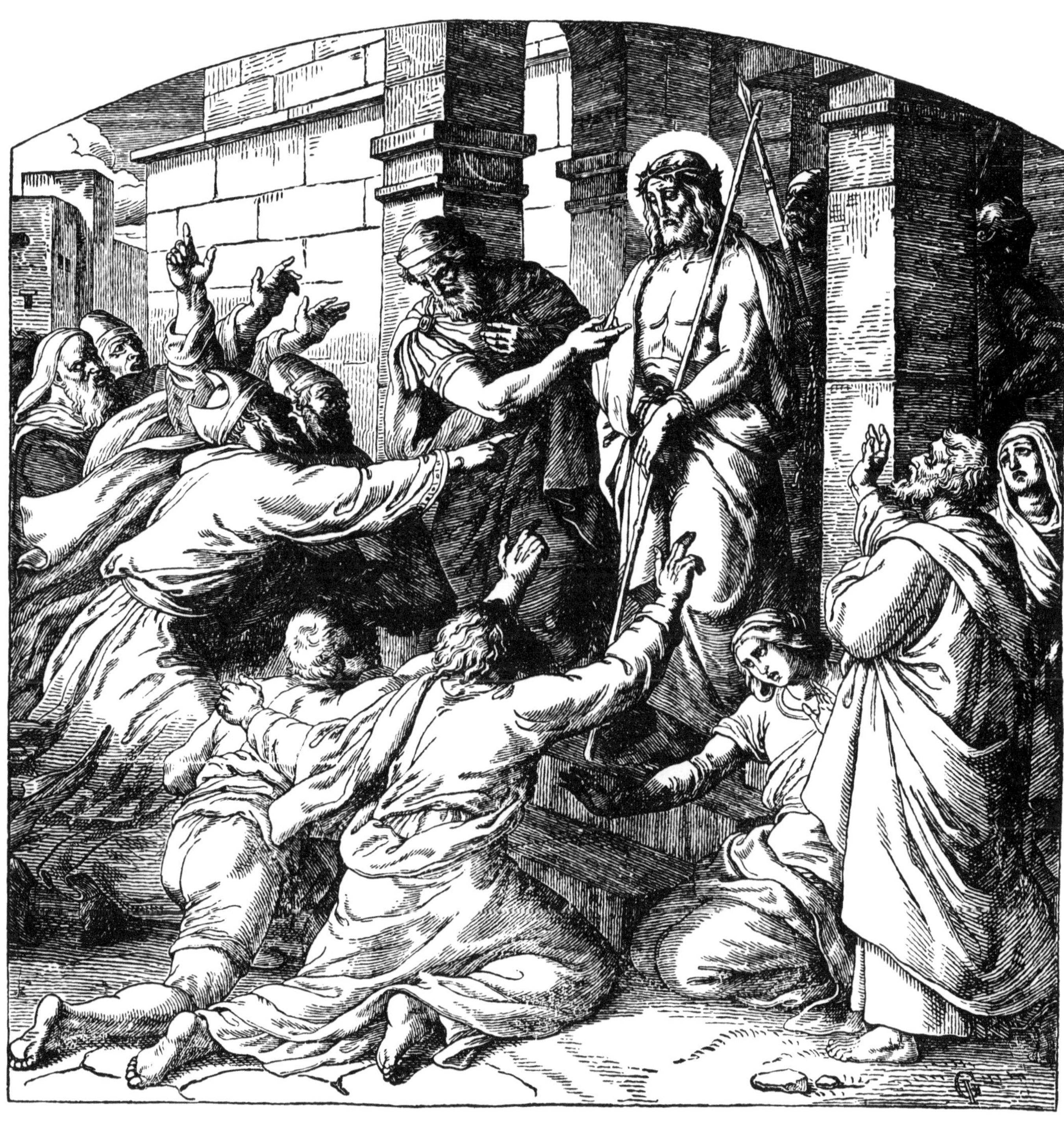

They Cried, "Crucify Him! Crucify Him!"

Pontius Pilate, the Roman Governor, could find no fault in Jesus and was unwilling to condemn him to death. So the chief priests cried out, We have found him perverting our nation, and forbidding to give tribute to Caesar, saying that he himself is Christ, a king. Pilate went back into the Judgment Hall, and said to Jesus, Art thou the King of the Jews?

Jesus answered, My kingdom is not of this world. But Pilate repeated his question, and then he said, I am a king. To this end was I born, and for this cause came I into the world, that I should bear witness to the truth. Then Pilate asked him, What is truth? But without waiting for an answer, he went out again to the chief priests, and said, I find no fault in him.

Pilate asked, What then will ye that I do unto him whom ye call the King of the Jews? the horrible cry arose, Crucify him, crucify him!

As soon as he could obtain silence, Pilate asked, Why, what evil hath he done? But they only cried out the more exceedingly, saying, Let him be crucified.

Pilate was unwilling to condemn Jesus to this terrible death, but it was now more difficult than ever to take the straightforward course which he ought to have adopted at the first, and he again gave way to cowardice, and tried half measures. Hoping that if some lesser punishment were inflicted upon Jesus, the people would be satisfied, he told his soldiers to lead away the prisoner into the hall called the Pretorium, and scourge him.

This was a cruel punishment, and the soldiers did not hesitate to add unnecessary cruelty, and cowardly insults. When the scourging was over, they again arrayed Jesus in the purple robe that Herod had put on him, and they twisted together a crown of thorns which they pressed upon his forehead, while in his hand they placed a reed instead of a sceptre. Then they all passed before him, one by one, and made a mock salute, calling out, Hail, King of the Jews! And as they did so, they spit upon him and smote him with the reed.

After this, they brought him back into the courtyard, faint and bleeding, and still wearing the crown of thorns and the purple robe. Pilate hoped that his enemies would now have pity, and would be willing to release him after this torture, but the chief priests had no pity. As soon as they saw him, they cried out again, Crucify him, crucify him!

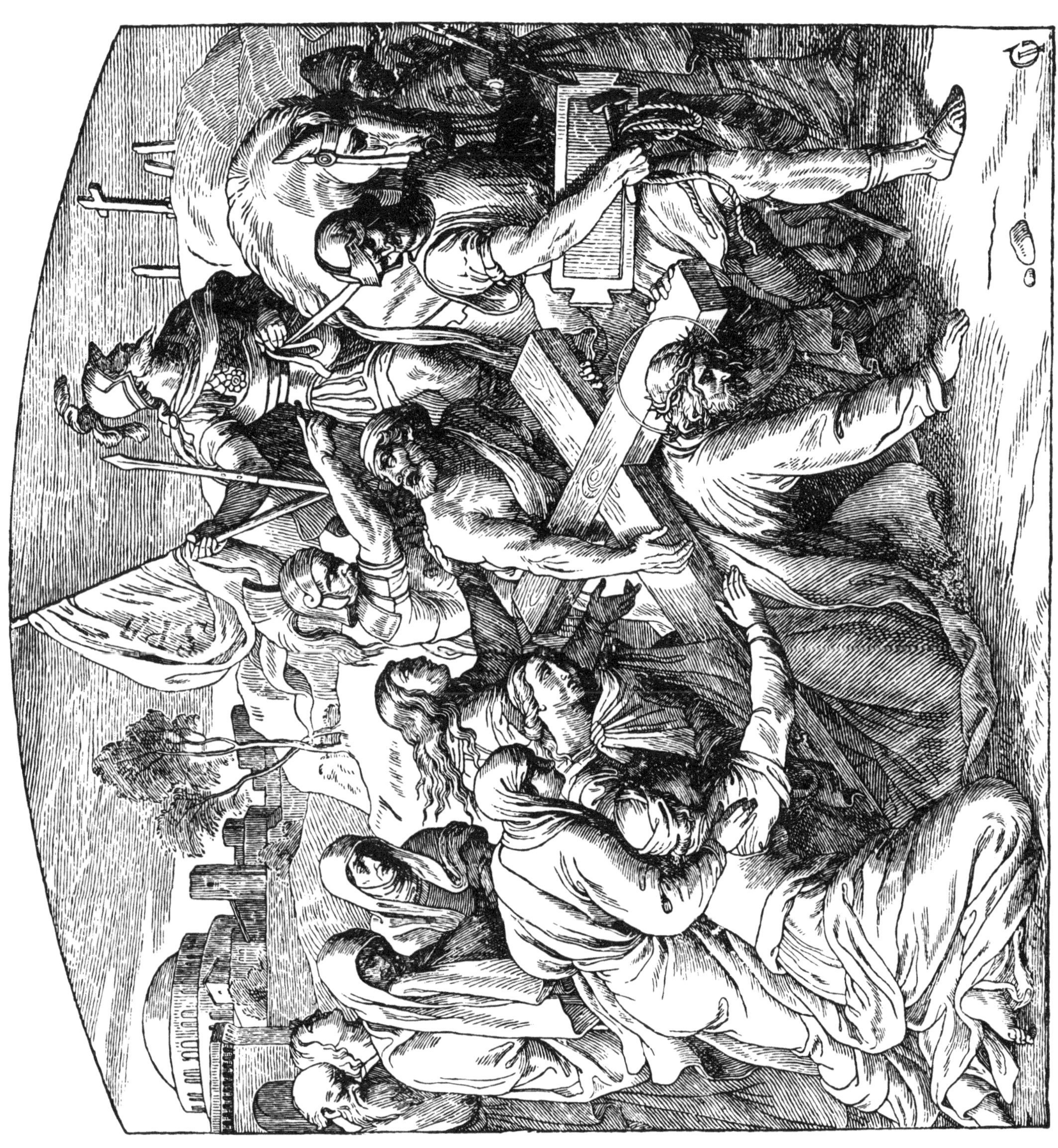

Simon Compelled to Help Jesus Bear the Cross

When a man was condemned by the Romans to the cruel death of crucifixion, it was the custom to make him carry the cross on which he was going to suffer, to the place of execution. As soon therefore as Pilate had given his cowardly consent to the demand of the chief priests, the soldiers stripped off from Jesus the gorgeous robe with which they had covered him in scorn, put his own clothes upon him, and laid the cross upon his shoulders.

The place of execution, which was called Golgotha, or Calvary, was outside the city walls, and Jesus went out towards it, bearing his cross, with a great multitude following after him. But he was weak and faint after the sleepless night, the agony in the garden, and all the pain he had already suffered, and he could not carry the heavy cross, so the soldiers seized upon a man named Simon the Cyrenian, whom they chanced to meet, and compelled him to carry the cross instead of Jesus.

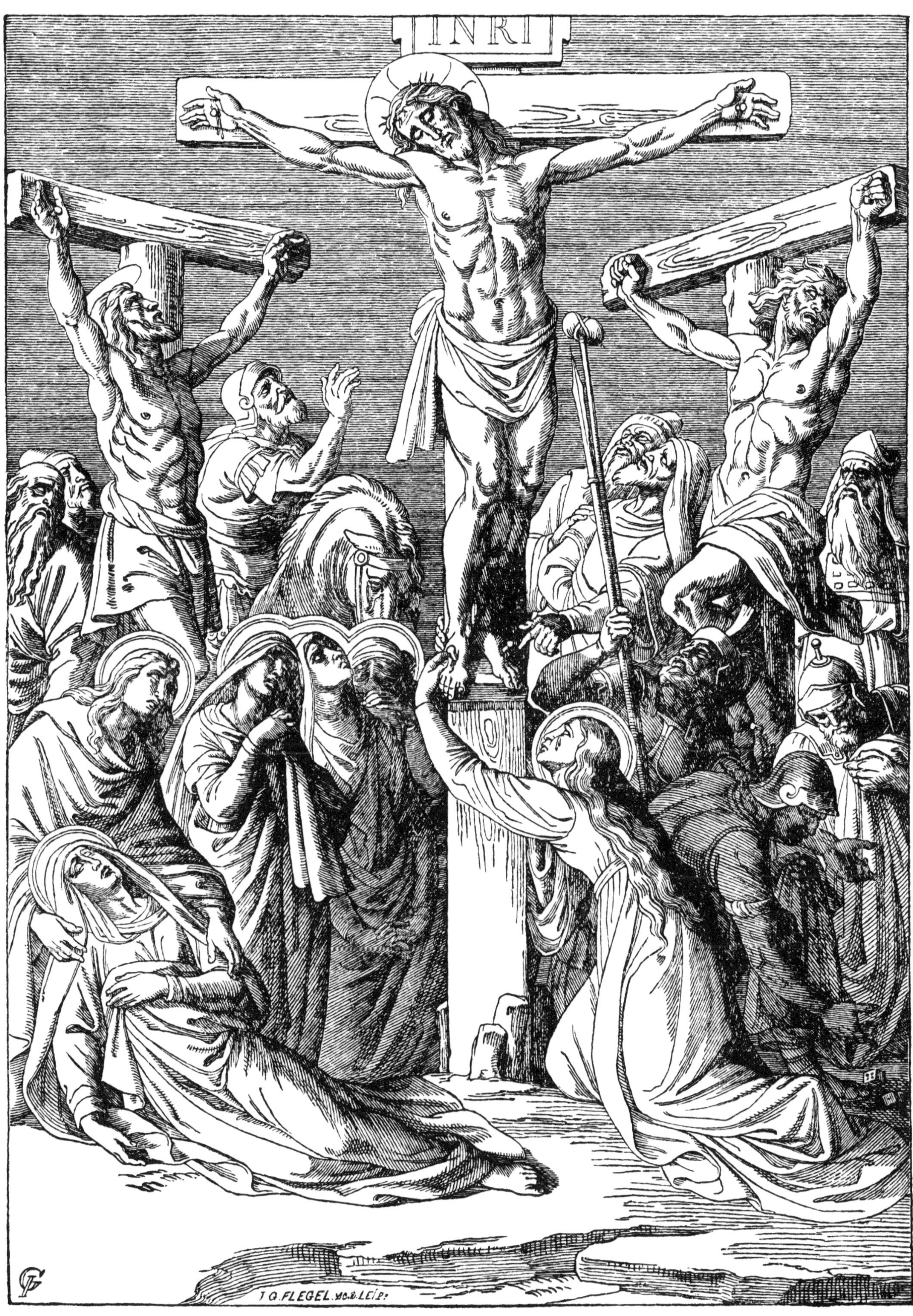
INRI
FLEGEL

The Crucifixion of Christ

At the place called Golgotha, or Calvary, the soldiers took Jesus and nailed his feet and hands to the cross. But even at that moment of terrible pain, only a prayer escaped from his lips: Father, forgive them, for they know not what they do.

Then the cross was raised up and set between two other crosses, on each of which there hung a thief. Over each cross was written the crime for which he who was upon it had been condemned to suffer, and over that of Jesus, were the words, The King of the Jews. He who above all men honored God, had been condemned by the chief priests for blasphemy; he who had made himself the least of all and the servant of all, was condemned by Pilate for claiming to be a king. A great crowd remained standing round the foot of the cross, and the chief priests, whose hearts were as hard as iron, continued to mock and revile Jesus. He saved others, they said; himself he cannot save. If he be the Christ, the King of Israel, let him now come down from the cross, and we will believe him. Even the two thieves who were hanging by his side joined in these scoffings, but Jesus heeded them not. His eye passed over the crowd till it rested upon the faces of his beloved disciple John, and his mother, Mary, who was there with some of the other women that had followed him from Galilee.

As always throughout his life, he thought not of himself but of others; and now that he was leaving those whom he had loved the most, it was well that they should love one another the more tenderly. He said to the disciple, Behold thy mother, and to his mother he said, Behold thy son. And from that hour, that disciple took her to his own home.

At midday, the sun hid the face of Jesus as he hung on the cross, and there fell upon the land a darkness which lasted for three hours. The scoffing crowd was hushed and filled with awe; and in silence Jesus endured the agony of those terrible hours in which he suffered for the sins of men, until just at the end of the time he uttered an exceeding bitter cry, My God, my God, why hast thou forsaken me?

But God had not forsaken him. Almost immediately the darkness rolled away from the face of the earth, and the cloud was removed from the soul of Jesus. Father, he said, into thy hands I commend my spirit! A few moments afterwards, he said, I thirst, and one of the soldiers filled a sponge with the sour wine or vinegar that they were accustomed to drink, and put it to his lips. He tasted it, and then with a loud cry, It is finished, he gave up his spirit.

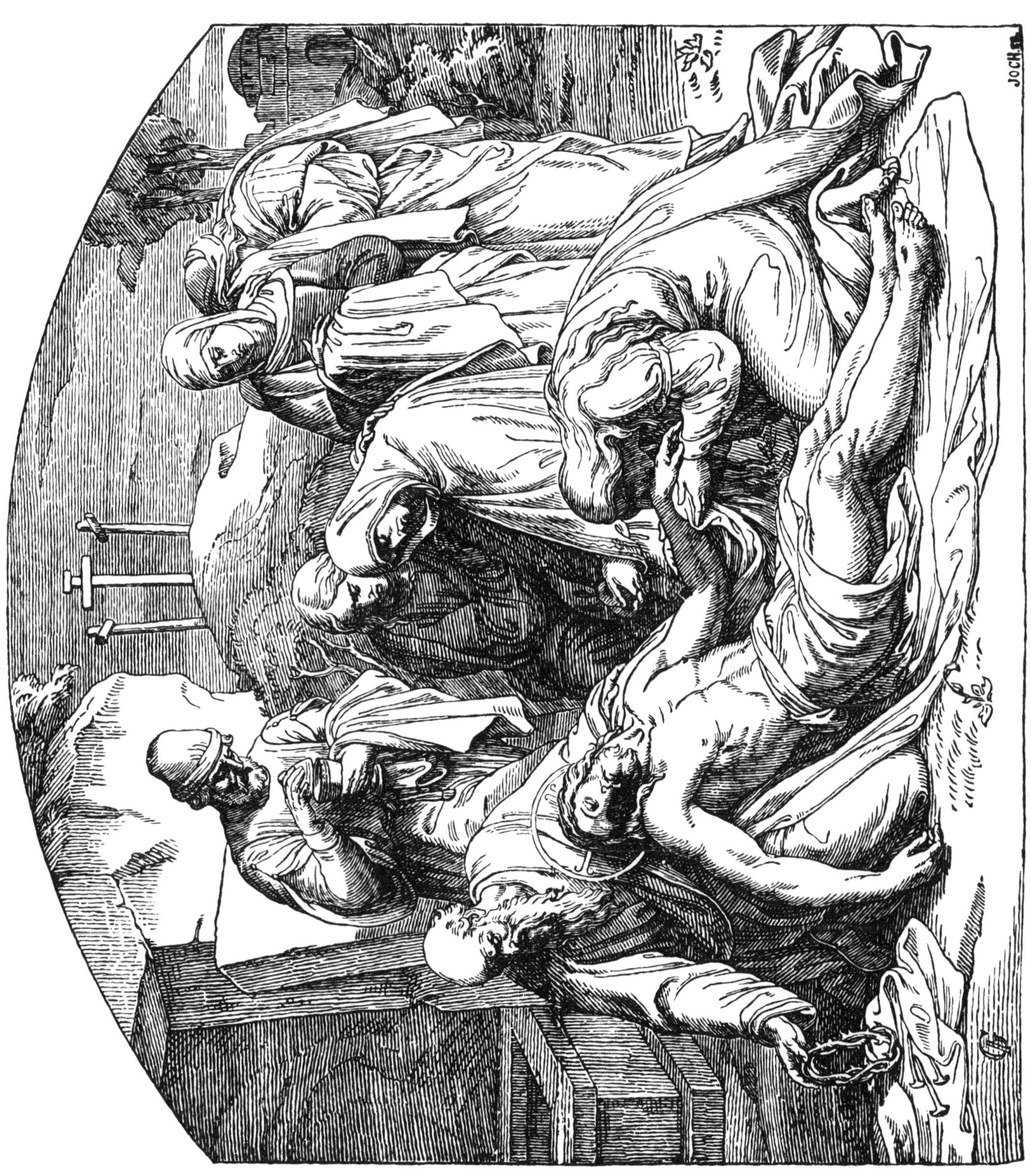

The Burial of Christ

Among the Pharisees, there were two men who had not consented to the death of Jesus. One of these was Joseph of Arimathea, a good man and a just; the other was Nicodemus. They had been unable to prevent the murder, but they could at least give the body an honorable burial; and Joseph went to Pilate, and asked to be allowed to take it down from the cross.

Pilate gave him leave, and he hurried back with a long piece of fine white linen, which he bought to wrap round the body. Joseph took down the body from the cross, with the help of the women who loved Jesus. They had been standing near it all the time, and now they were anxious to see what would be done. It was the day which we call Friday, and at six o'clock that evening the Jewish Sabbath would begin, on which no one was allowed to do any work, so that there was but little time for the burial.

In accordance with the Jewish custom of anointing the bodies of those they desired to honor, Nicodemus had brought sweet-smelling spices and ointments; but all that could now be done was to wind the fine linen round the body, cover it with the spices, and lay it for the present in a garden close by that belonged to Joseph. In the garden there was a new tomb which had been hewn out of the rock; here they laid the body and closed up the entrance by rolling a great stone in front of it.

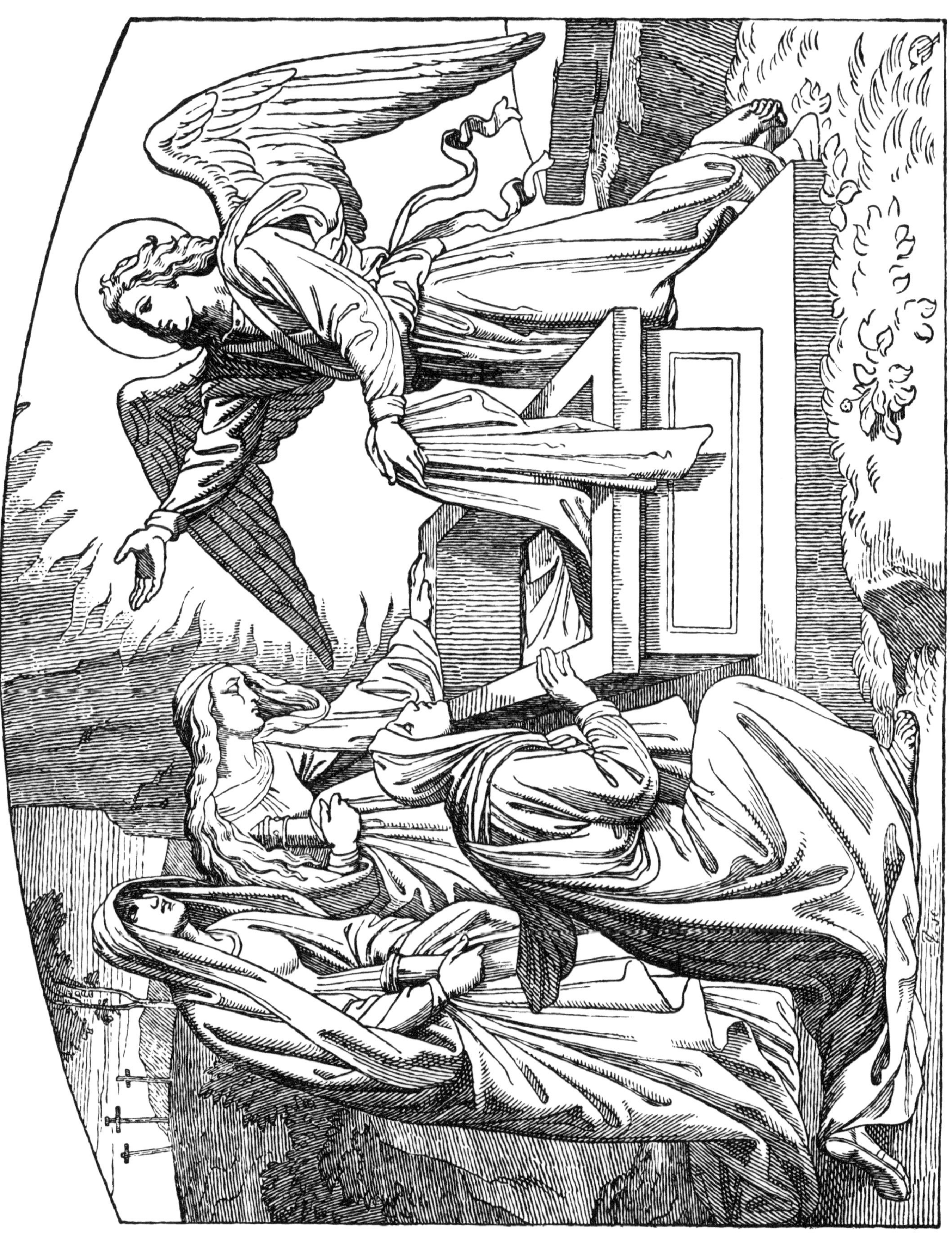

The Angel and Women at the Empty Tomb

The women who loved Jesus had risen very early upon the first day of the week, while it was yet dark, and went to the sepulchre, carrying with them the spices and ointments that they had prepared. But when they had reached the place, they found that the stone was gone. A great earthquake had shaken the garden, and an angel of the Lord had descended from heaven, and had rolled away the stone from the door of the sepulchre, and sat upon it. His countenance was like lightning, and his raiment white as snow. The women were frightened when they saw the angel, but he said unto them, Fear ye not, for I know that ye seek Jesus who was crucified. He is not here, for he is risen, as he said. Come, see the place where the Lord lay. And go quickly, and tell his disciples that he is risen from the dead. This was indeed a wonderful message, and the hearts of the women beat high with fear and great joy as they departed quickly from the sepulchre and ran to take the good news to the disciples.

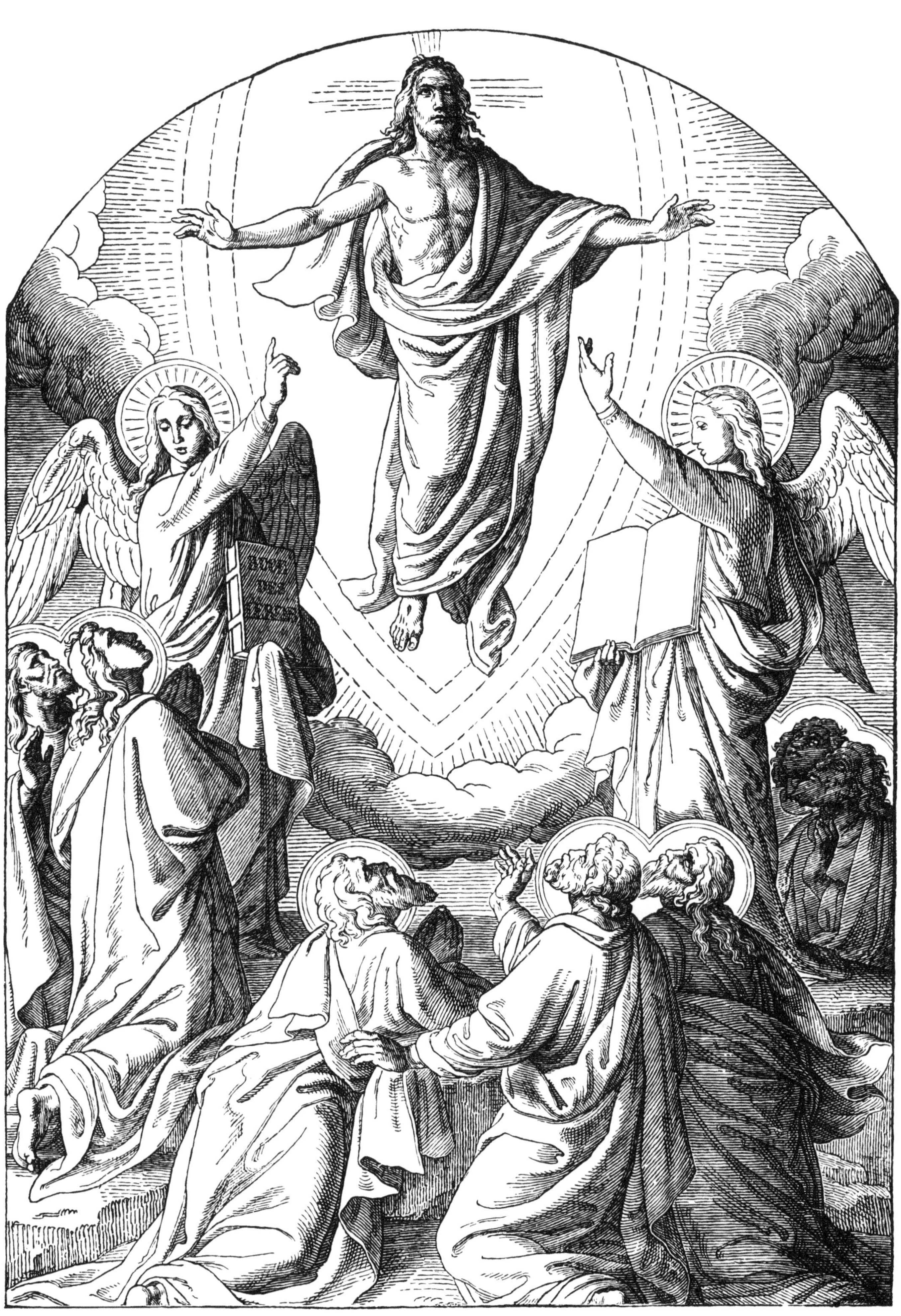

The Acension of Christ

It was now some weeks since the day when Jesus had risen from the dead, and the disciples had once more left Galilee and returned to Jerusalem, for their Master had told them that he would meet them there. At the time appointed he came, and he led them out from the city as far as to Bethany, the village on the Mount of Olives that he loved so well, the home of his friends, Martha and Mary and Lazarus.

As they went, he told them that the time had come when he must be parted from them, and they would see him no more, but that though he would no longer be with them in bodily presence, he would always be near them in spirit. He said, too, that he did not wish them to return to their homes or their fishing boats, but rather to devote the rest of their lives to the work that he himself had begun, and to go about teaching the good news of the kingdom of God, healing the sick, and casting out devils. He told them also, that he would prepare them for this great work by pouring out upon them his Spirit of truth and holiness, and that after he had left them they were to return to Jerusalem, and wait for this Spirit to descend into their hearts. When they had received it, they were to begin and teach, first in Jerusalem, and then in all other countries. Go ye and teach all nations, he said, baptizing them in the name of the Father, and of the Son, and of the Holy Ghost, teaching them to observe all things, whatsoever I have commanded you. And, lo! I am with you always, even unto the end of the world.

When Jesus had ended these sayings, he lifted up his hands over his disciples, and blessed them. And it came to pass, that while he blessed them he was parted from them and carried up into heaven, and a cloud received him out of their sight.

The disciples knew that he would never again appear to them in bodily form, either at the breaking of bread, or by the seashore, or as they talked by the way; and yet they were filled, not with sorrow, but with great joy. Their Lord had conquered death, and had gone before them into the unseen world, with the promise on his lips that he would always be with them, and would send his Spirit to guide and comfort them.

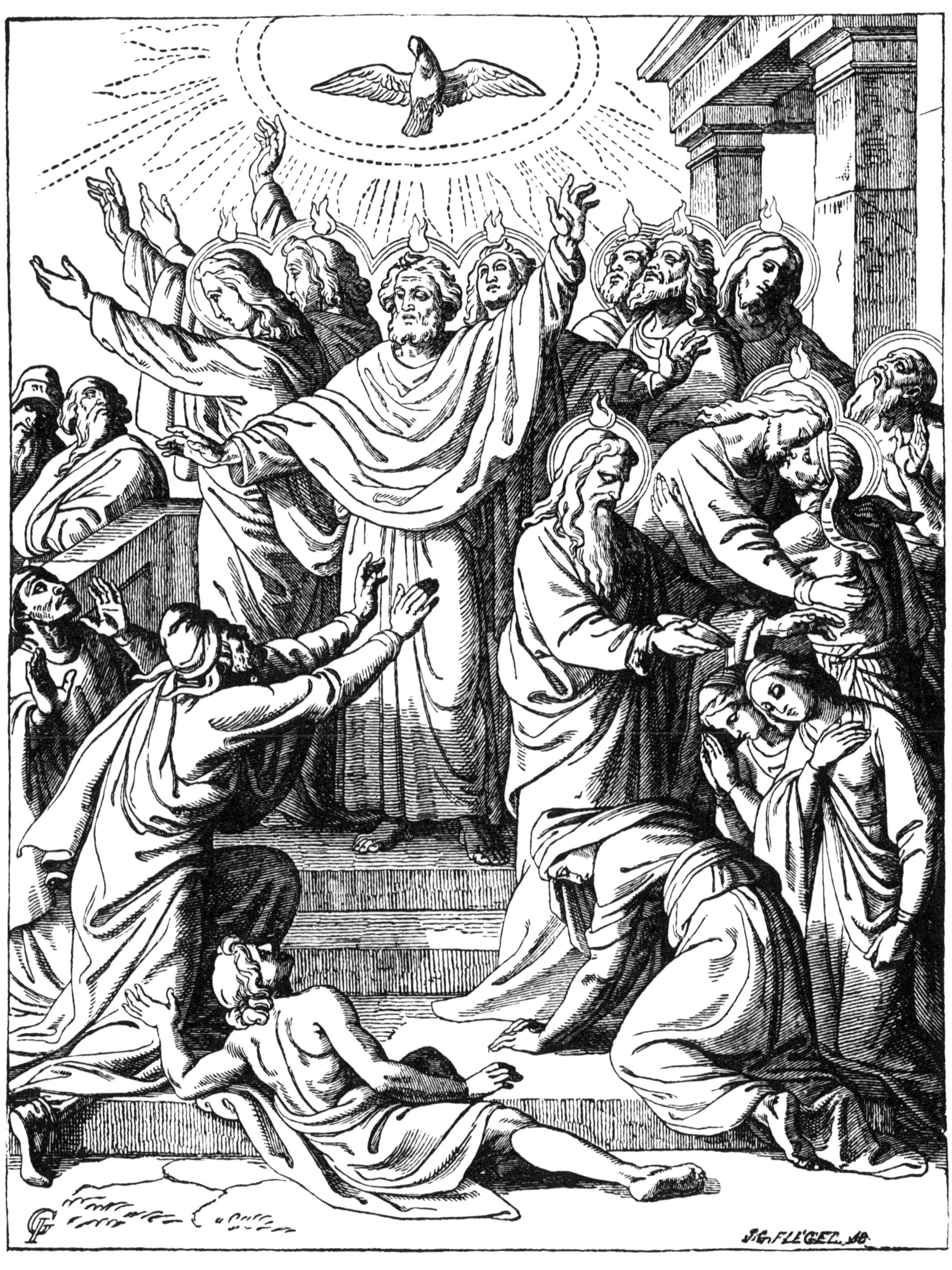
J.G.FLEGEL.

Tongues of Fire Resting on the Disciples

It was now fifty days after the Passover and the first day of the week. On this day the believers in Jesus met together in a large room to pray. It was early in the morning — about eight o'clock. Suddenly a great sound was heard. It was like the sound of a very strong, high wind. This great sound filled the place where the believers were sitting, and shook the whole house. There came also what looked like fire — divided into many parts, each part appearing to be a tongue of fire; and these came and sat on each of the believers — on the women as well as on the men. At the same time they all were able to speak many strange languages which they had never learned. Jesus had once told his apostles to preach the Gospel to every creature, and they may have wondered how they should be able to teach strange nations; but now they were made able to speak to every one in his own language.

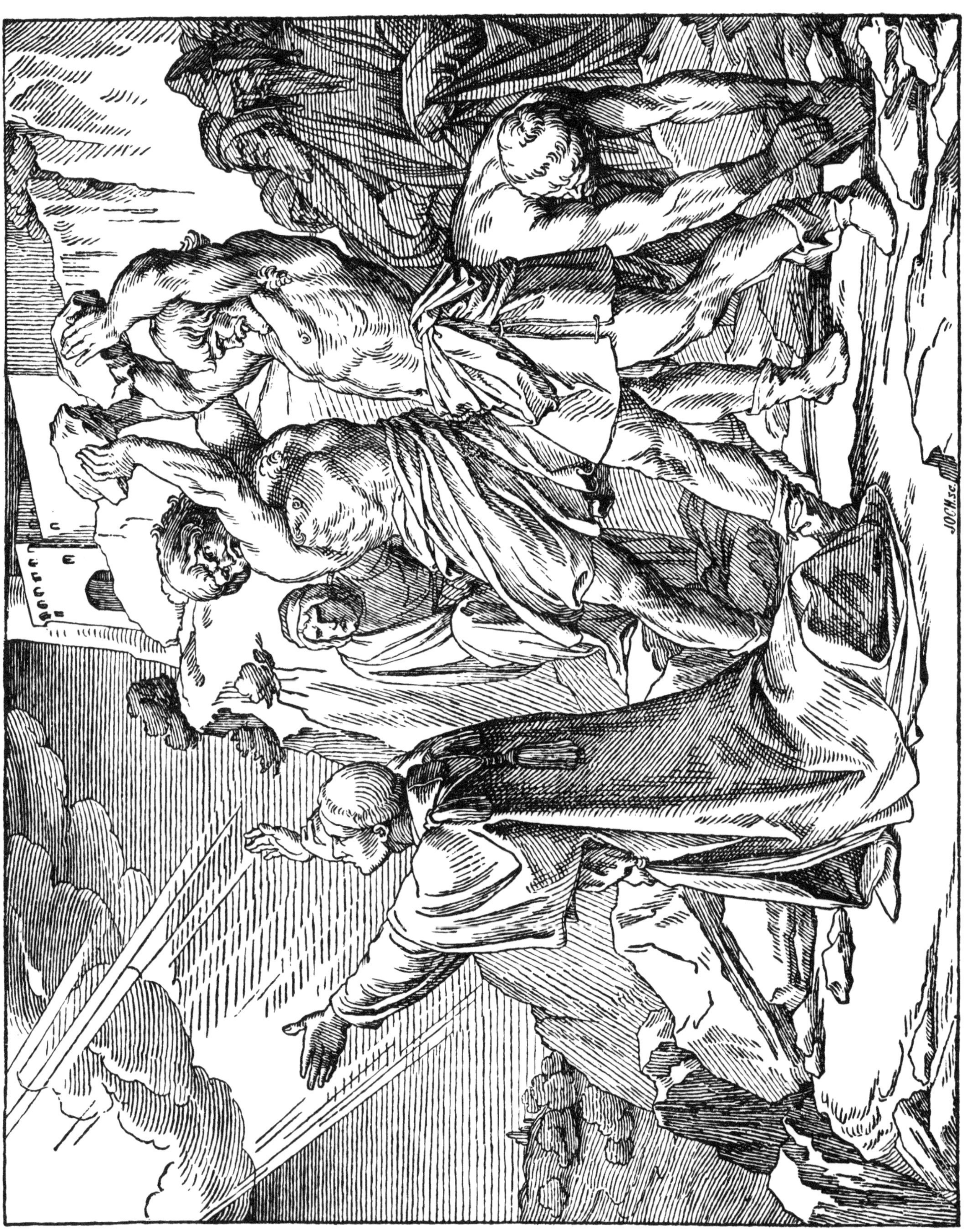

Stephen Stoned to Death by His Enemies

Seven men were to be called deacons, or servants, for they were to help the apostles. And the chief of the seven was named Stephen, a holy and a wise man. He was full of faith, and did great wonders among the people. But the enemies of Jesus hated him the more for being so wonderful. Learned Jews went to him and disputed with him, but they found that Stephen was wiser than they were. So they determined to bring him before the great council, called the Sanhedrim, and to bribe men to tell lies of him. And they went about among the people, and set the people against him by saying false things of him. False witnesses came in and said that Stephen had declared that Jesus of Nazareth would destroy the temple though Stephen had never said this, for it would be the Romans who would destroy the temple.

After Stephen had been so falsely accused, the judges, who sat round, looked at him, and were surprised to see his face like the face of an angel, so bright, so glorious, so holy. But this sight did not turn the hearts of the wicked judges. They went on judging him.

The high priest, after hearing the wicked men accuse him, said to Stephen, Are these things so? Then Stephen began to defend himself against what the false witnesses had said of him. He made a very long speech; at last he told his judges that all of them had been murderers of the Son of God.

This made the judges very angry. Stephen's words cut them to the heart, but did not make them repent. They gnashed upon him with their teeth. They were like devils; he was like an angel. He lifted up his eyes toward heaven, and saw there the glory of God and Jesus standing on his right hand. Then he cried out, Behold, I see the heavens opened, and Jesus standing on the right hand of God.

Then they cried out with a loud voice, and stopped their ears, that they might not hear Stephen's blessed words, and they ran upon him all together, as the men of Nazareth had once hunted Jesus. They ran beside the temple courts, along the street that led to a gate of the city; and when they had got Stephen out, they took up great stones and threw them at him.

Stephen went on praying as the stones were falling, calling out, Lord Jesus, receive my spirit. At last, when bruised all over and ready to die, he kneeled down and said, Lord, lay not this sin to their charge. Thus with his last breath he asked God to forgive his cruel murderers. As soon as he had offered this prayer he fell asleep. This was the death of the first martyr.

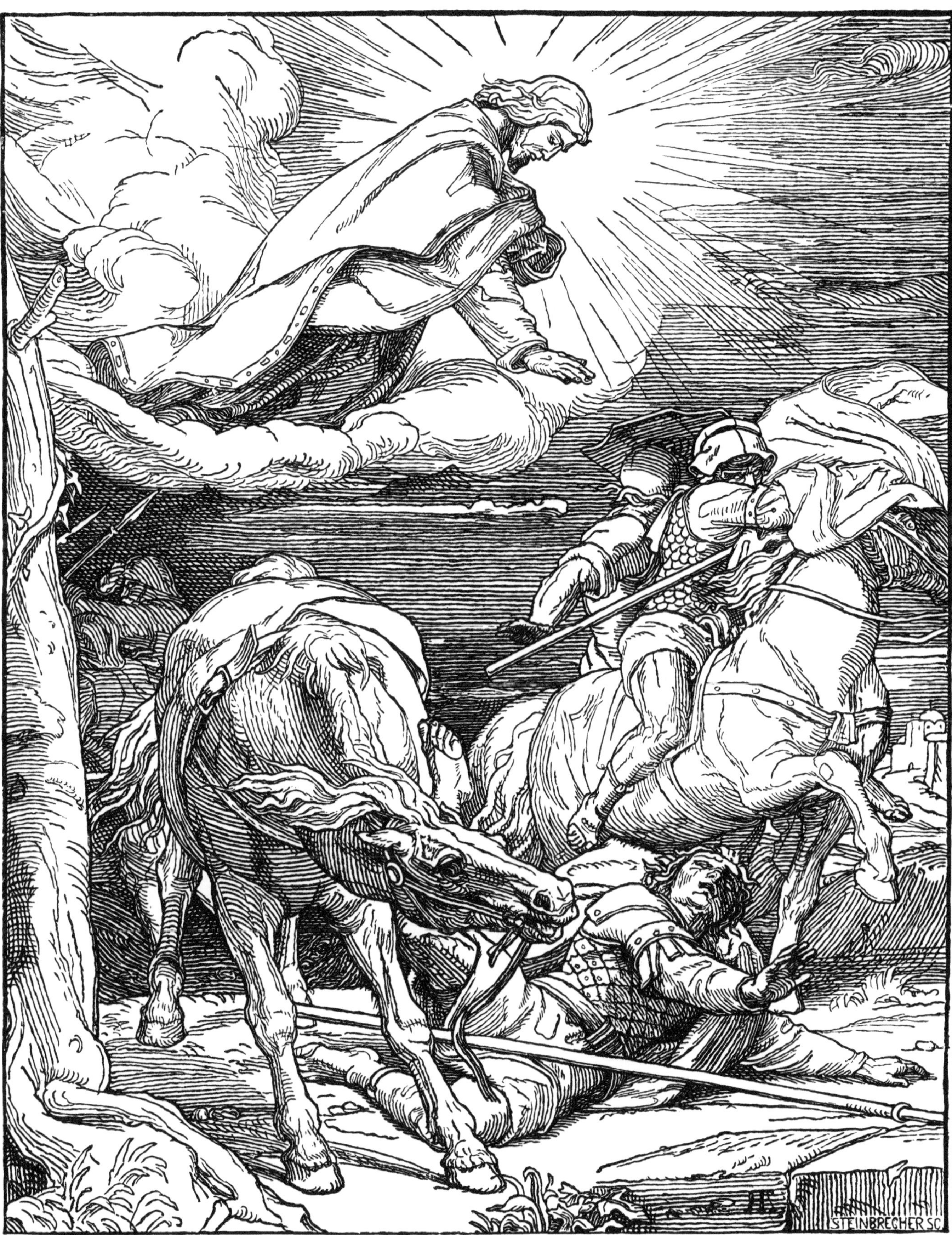
STEINBRECHER SC.

Saul Struck to the Earth on His Way to Damascus

There was a young man named Saul, who treated cruelly the disciples of Jesus. This young man thought he did right in ill-treating believers in Christ, for he thought Christ was a deceiver, and not really the Son of God. After he had done much harm in Jerusalem, he went to other cities to hurt the believers who lived in them. He set out for Damascus to seize the believers there, and to bring them in chains to Jerusalem.

Saul was travelling with several men as his guard. They all arrived in sight of Damascus about noonday, when the sun is the brightest. Suddenly there appeared a light from heaven, brighter than the sun. This light was so dazzling that all the travellers fell down with their faces to the ground, quite unable to look up.

While thus lying down, Saul heard a voice from heaven, saying, Saul, Saul, why dost thou persecute me? Saul answered, Who art thou, Lord? The voice replied, I am Jesus, whom thou persecutest. Saul, still trembling and astonished, inquired, Lord, what wouldst thou have me to do? The voice replied, Arise, and go into the city, and it shall be told thee what thou must do. Saul did not get up until Jesus said, Rise, and stand upon thy feet. Then Saul arose, and opened his eyes, but behold! he could not see! the dazzling light had blinded him!

As he sat in darkness, Saul was thinking of his sins against Jesus, and of his cruelty to his people. And in this sad state of blindness and misery, God sent him a dream that was comforting. Saul saw a man in his dream whose name was Ananias. He came, and put his hands on Saul, and said, Receive thy sight.

Then Ananias went to Saul, and put his hands on him, and said, Brother Saul, the Lord Jesus, who appeared to you, has sent me to you, that you may receive your sight. As he said this, something like skin fell from Saul's eyes, and Saul found he was able to see.

Saul stayed a good while in Damascus, and he became great friends with all the people of the Lord in that city. Those very people that he once meant to send to prison were now his dearest friends. He went to the synagogues, and preached there about Jesus Christ, that he was the Son of God.

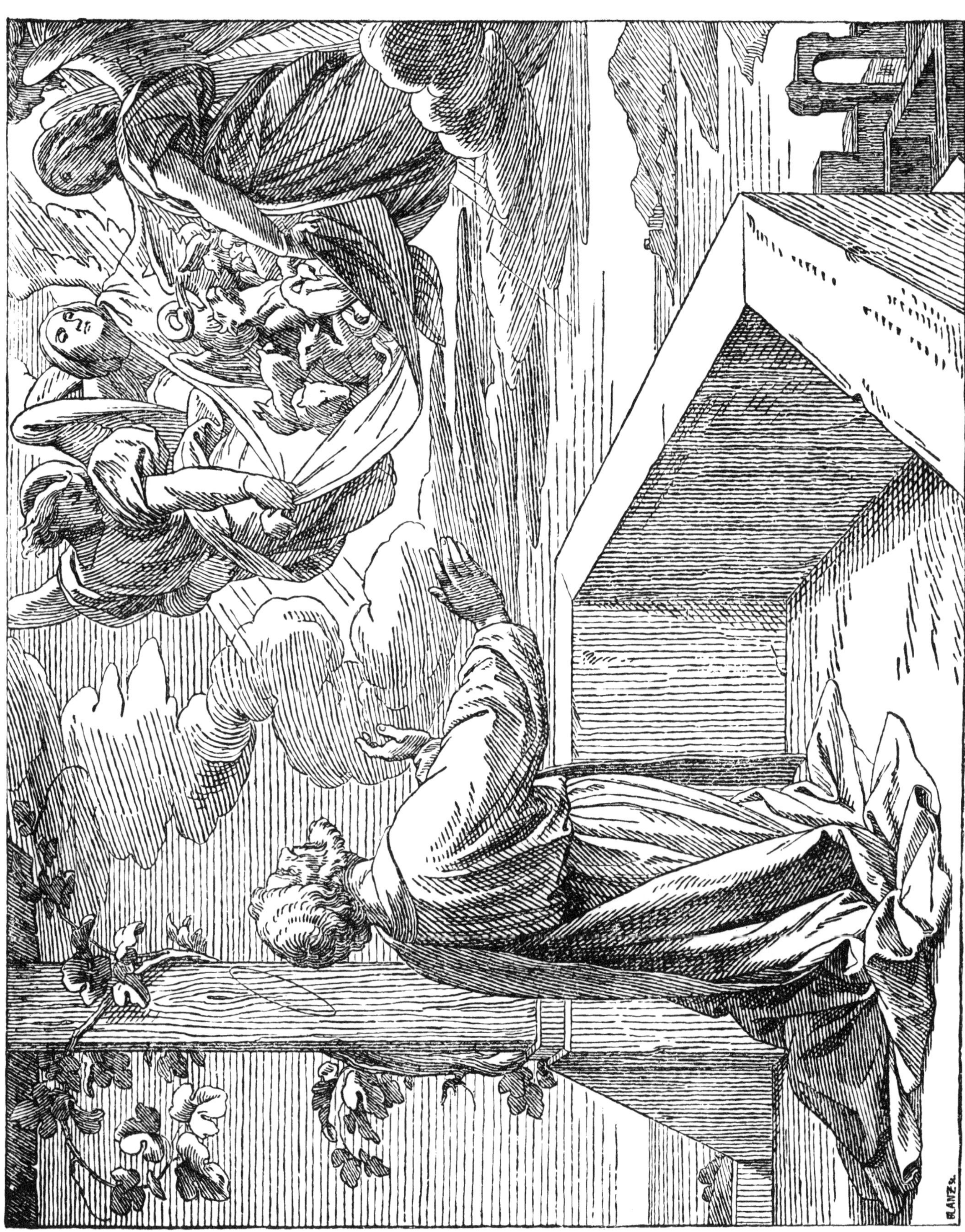

Peter's Vision on the Housetop

While Peter was living at Joppa he lodged with Simon the tanner. He went up one day to the top of the house, which was flat. He wanted to be alone to pray to God. After awhile, he fell into a sort of sleep and had a very strange dream. He thought that the sky was opened, and that there was let down out of it a great sheet, with the four corners fastened, so that the sheet could hold things. Inside there were all kinds of four-footed beasts, and some of them were wild; and all kinds of birds, and all kinds of creeping things.

Then Peter heard a voice, saying, Rise, Peter, kill and eat. Peter was surprised at hearing this command, for God had given the Jews very strict rules about eating. He had forbidden them to eat of beasts called unclean, such as pigs, hares, horses, and donkeys. Among birds he had forbidden the Jews to eat of eagles, owls, swans, storks, and many others; and also he had forbidden them to eat of creeping things, lizards, snails, and moles.

So when Peter had looked well at these unclean animals, he answered the voice, Not so, Lord; for I have never eaten anything that is common or unclean. The voice from heaven replied, Whatever God has made clean, call not thou common. Three times the voice spoke these words, and then the great sheet of animals was taken up again into heaven.

When the dream was over, Peter went on thinking about it, and wondering the meaning of it. At that time the Spirit spoke to his mind, saying, Three men are come to your house, and they want you to go with them. Go with them, for I have sent them. Then Peter went down the stairs from the housetop, and he found three men waiting to see him, just as the Spirit had told him. He said to them, I am the person you want to see. Why are you come for me?

Then the three men replied: Cornelius, a very good man, was told by a holy angel to send for you to come to his house, that you might tell him how he may be saved.

Peter found that these three men were the servants of Cornelius, and that Cornelius was a great captain. The three men were not Jews; and Cornelius, the master, was not a Jew. They were all Romans. Now the Jews called all other nations Gentiles; and they despised them all as common or unclean. Peter saw why the dream had been sent to him; he saw that God did not call these men common or unclean. So Peter promised to go with them.

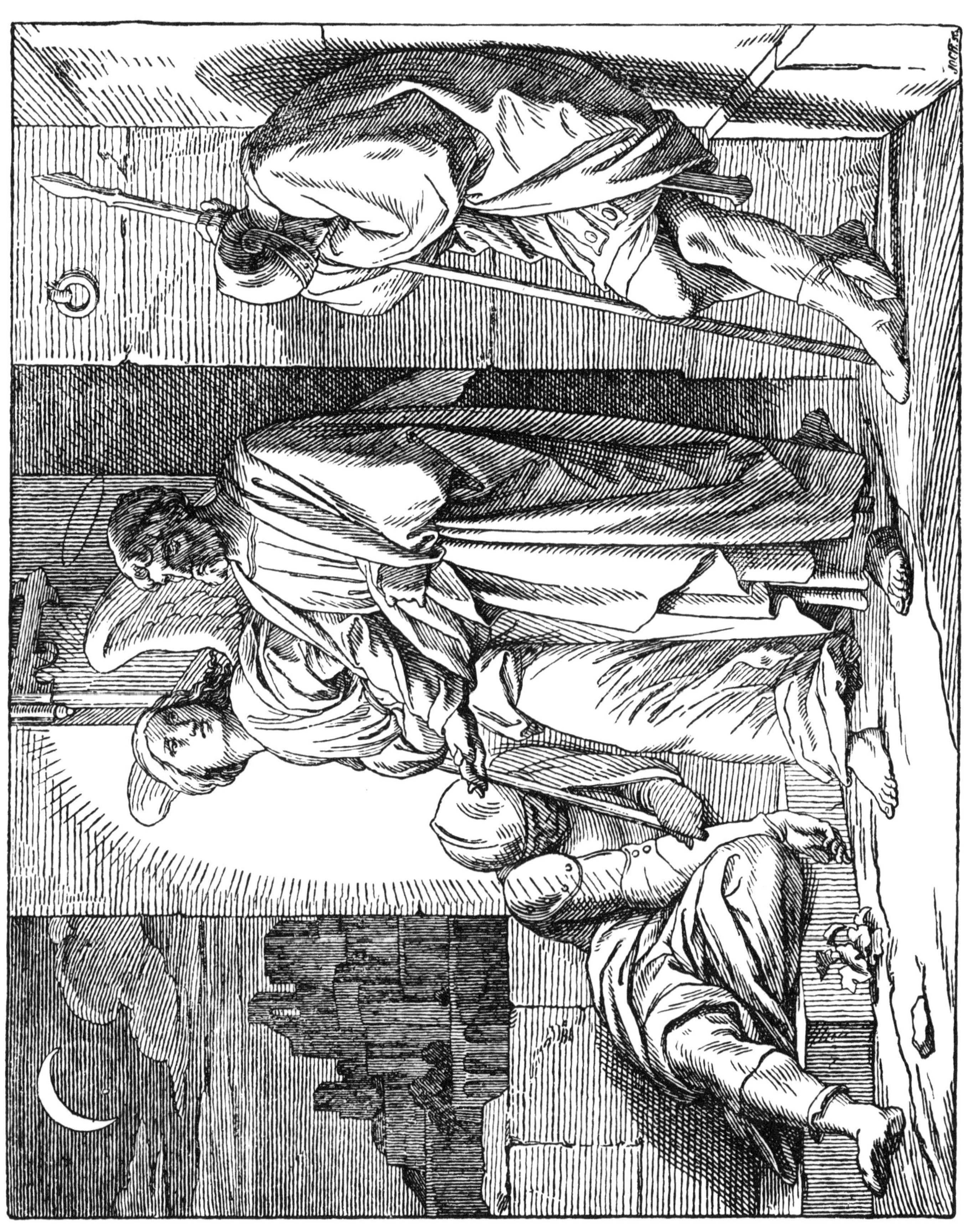

Peter Delivered from Prison by an Angel

At this time, the wicked King Herod imprisoned Peter and planned to kill him. But, as Herod had heard of Peter once escaping from prison, he ordered sixteen soldiers to guard him night and day.

The night before Peter was to be killed, a group of saints met together to pray for him while Peter was quietly sleeping in prison. Each of Peter's hands was fastened to a soldier's hand on each side of him. Suddenly an angel made the dark prison brighter than the day. Yet Peter was so sound asleep that he did not wake till the angel touched him, saying, Arise up quickly. And as Peter rose up, the chains fell off his hands. All this time the soldiers slept.

The angel said, Follow me. Peter followed, feeling as if he were dreaming. The angel led him past many soldiers that had been placed to watch outside, and brought him to the great iron gate. Though it had bolts and bars, it opened without key and without hand, as if it had opened itself. The angel brought him down one street, and then departed. When Peter found himself alone, he stopped to think of what had happened. He saw that God had set him free and saved him from death.

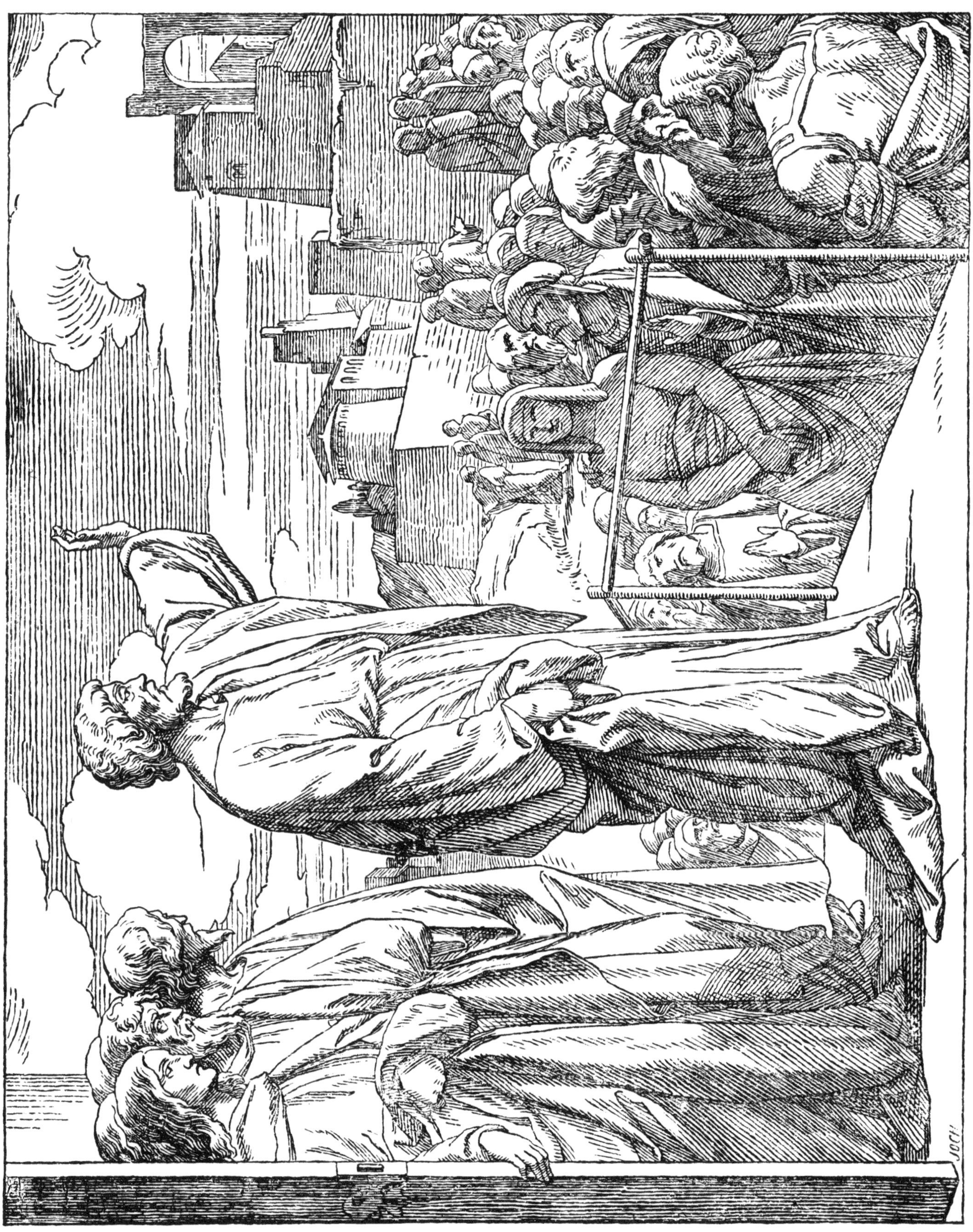

Paul Preaching on Mars' Hill

There were many wise heathens in Athens who were always in the marketplace, talking and teaching. Paul went there to talk with them and to teach them about Jesus. These pretended wise men laughed at Paul, and called him a fool. Some were offended and said, He wants to set up new gods. But at last they proposed a plan which pleased Paul. These Athenians were fond of hearing new things, so they thought they should like to hear Paul preach about the new things he told them. They led him up a hill in the city to a temple where Mars, the god of war, was worshipped.

Paul stood up on Mars' Hill to speak of the Prince of Peace. He spoke first of the one true God, who made all things, and of the sin of worshipping idols. He said God commanded them to repent, and that he would judge the world one day by Christ whom he had raised from the dead. This is what he said: Ye men of Athens, I perceive that in all things ye are too superstitious. For as I passed by, and beheld your devotions, I found an altar with this inscription, To The Unknown God. Whom therefore ye ignorantly worship, him declare I unto you.

God that made the world and all things therein, seeing that he is Lord of heaven and earth, dwelleth not in temples made with hands; neither is worshipped with men's hands, as though he needed any thing, seeing he giveth to all life, and breath, and all things; and hath made of one blood all nations of men for to dwell on all the face of the earth, and hath determined the times before appointed, and the bounds of their habitation; that they should seek the Lord, if haply they might feel after him, and find him, though he be not far from every one of us: for in him we live, and move, and have our being, for we are also his offspring.

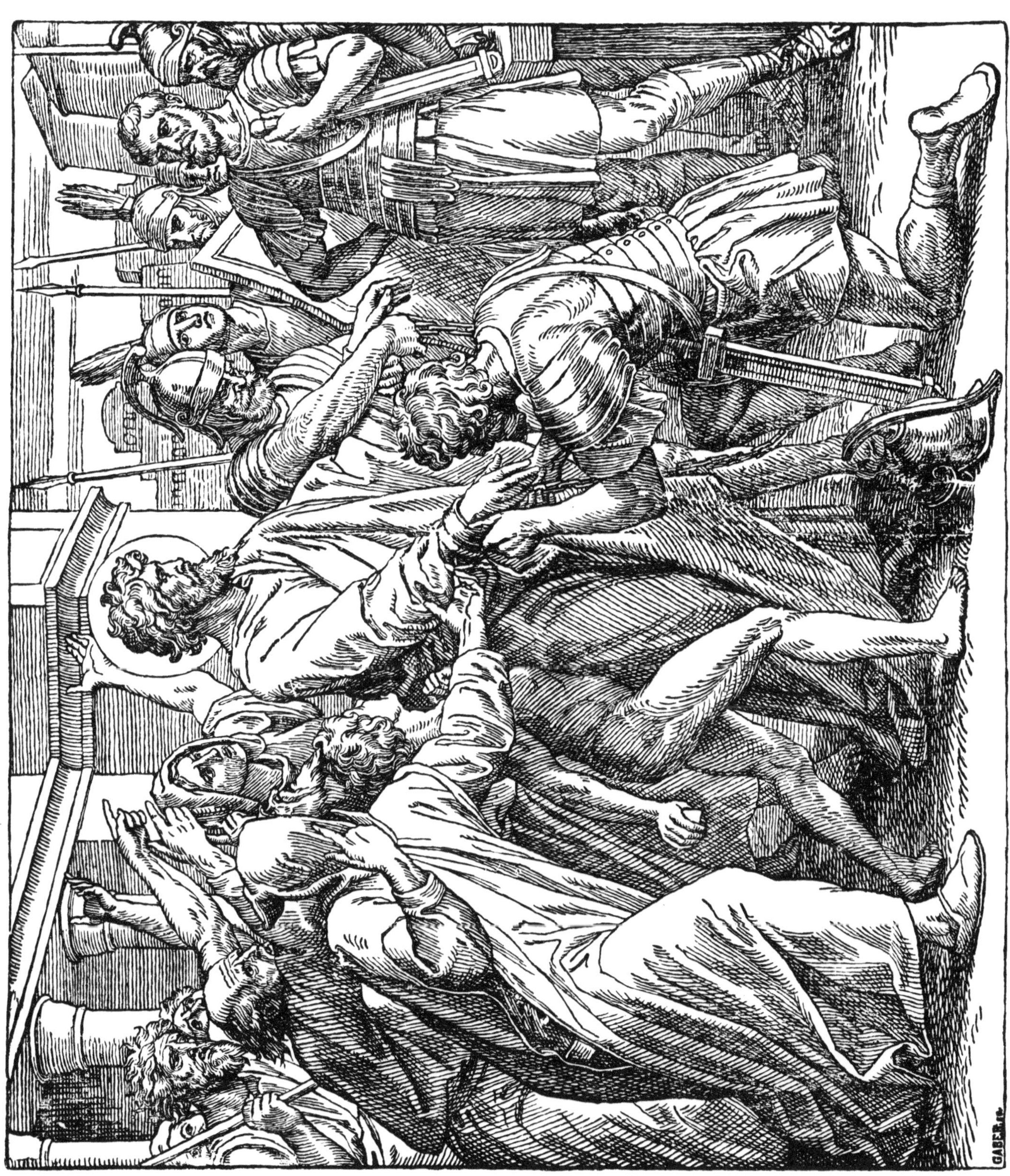

Paul Bound with Chains

The famous apostle Paul came to Jerusalem, and the day after his arrival, a great meeting was held. Paul addressed the assembly, telling the history of his travels, and of how God had turned the hearts of many Gentiles from idols to Jesus. Praises flowed from the lips of the believers when Paul had finished his speech!

Then some elders arose and gave the apostle their advice: Brother, show that you honor the law of Moses by doing what we desire. We have here four men who have made a vow, probably the vow of the Nazarite; see that they shave their heads, and let them purify themselves with you. Thus you will show thousands of Jews that you keep the law, and teach the Jews to keep it.

Paul followed this advice and took the men into the temple, for they were Jews. The men were purified during seven days. When the seven days were almost over, some Jews from Asia, seeing Paul in the temple, stirred up the people against him, and seized him, and told lies saying, This Paul is the man who goes about speaking against the temple; and he has now taken Gentiles into the temple.

Most people believed what the Jews from Asia said; and they all ran together into the temple. They found Paul, and seized hold of him, and dragged him out into the streets, and would soon have stoned him had they not suddenly stopped in their wickedness.

There was a great tower, just above the temple, where a thousand Roman soldiers lodged. The captain heard that there was an uproar in the city, and he ran down in haste, with many soldiers, to the place where Paul was. He found the Jews beating him, but when these men saw the captain, they left off beating Paul; for they knew they had no right to do so. The chief captain came near, and ordered his soldiers to bind Paul with chains.

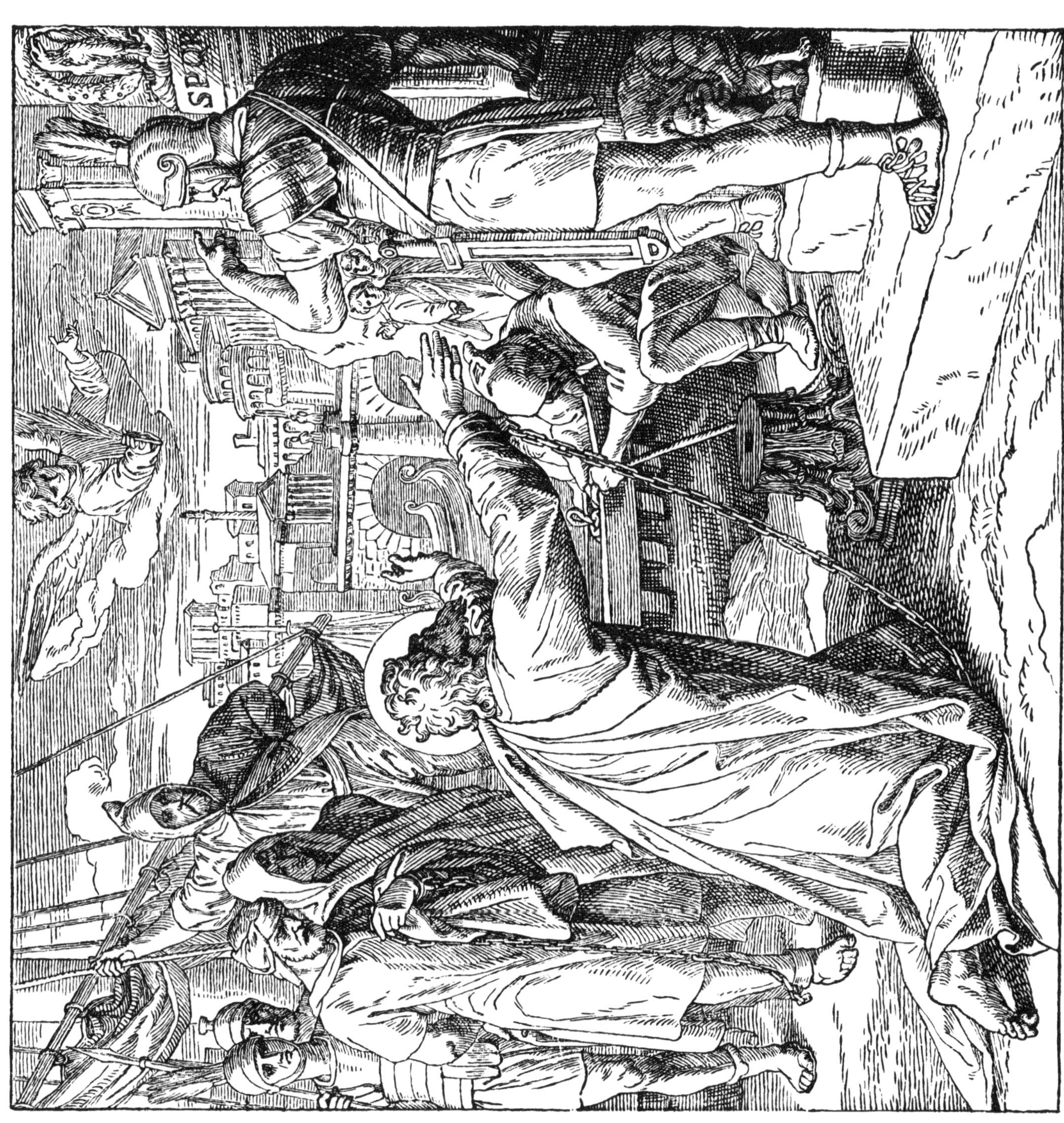

ST. PAUL'S ARRIVAL AT ROME IN CHAINS

Paul was given into the charge of a centurion named Julius and the centurion hired a ship to take his whole company to Rome. The ship sailed to the shores of Italy till it came to a fine harbor called Puteoli, more than a hundred miles from Rome. Here Paul landed, still chained to a soldier, and accompanied by friends.

The day came for the centurion to lead his prisoner to Rome. He took him along a well-paved road, very near the seacoast. On the road Paul met some friends who had come from Rome on purpose to welcome him. Seeing them pleased his heart so much that he thanked God and took courage. At last he arrived at Rome, with a troop of loving friends around him, as well as the soldier to whom he was chained.

The chief Jews were soon on the way to see Paul. They had often heard of him, but very few had ever seen him; and they must have longed to see such a wonderful man. They found him weak and worn, chained to a soldier, bowed down with age and sorrow, but full of love and kindness.

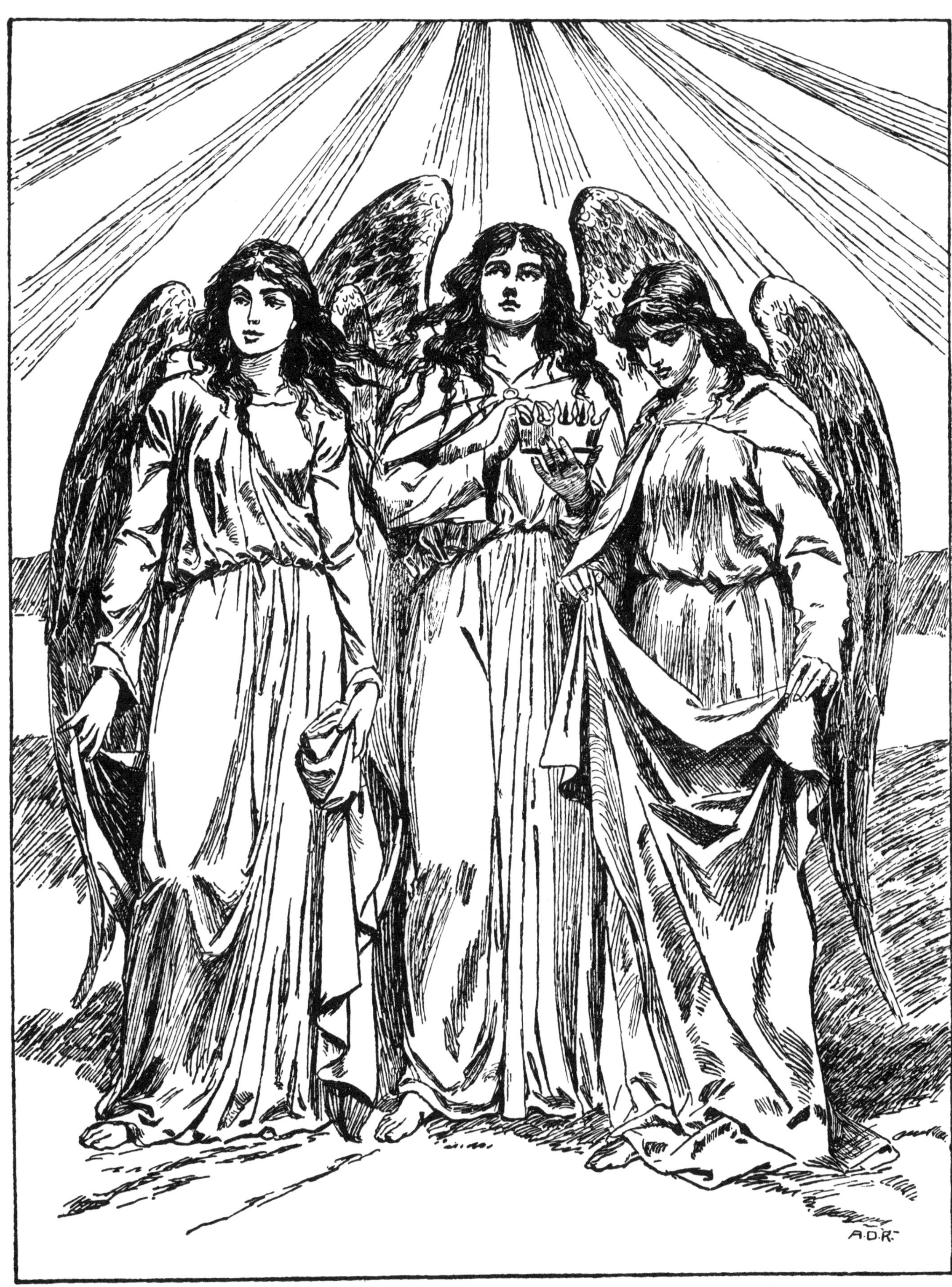
A.D.R.

Faith, Hope and Charity

Faith, Hope and Charity, of heavenly birth,
bestow the richest blessings known to Earth.

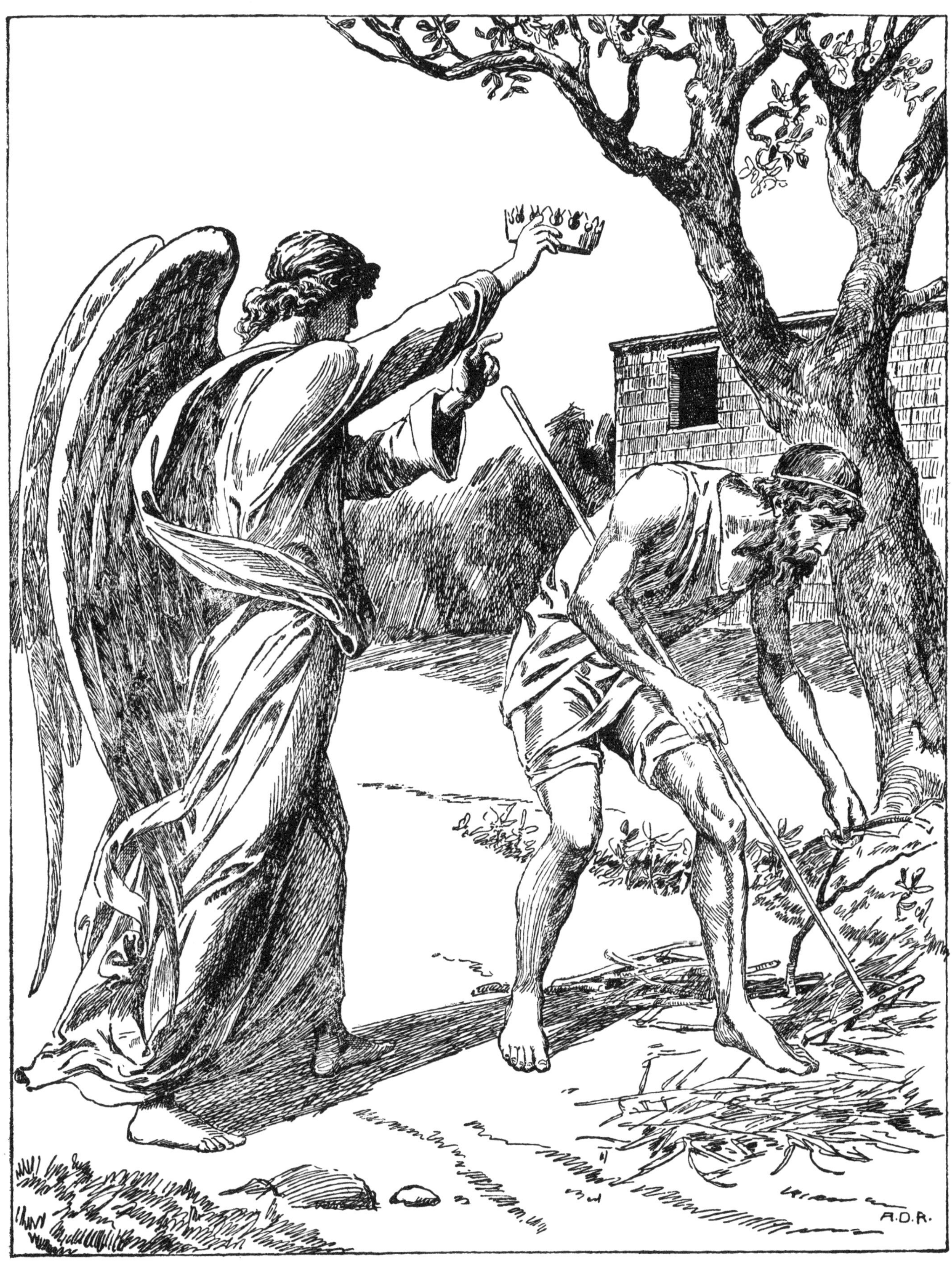
A.D.R.

Not For a Crown

Not for a crown will this poor worldling pause,
But wastes his life in gathering sticks and straws.

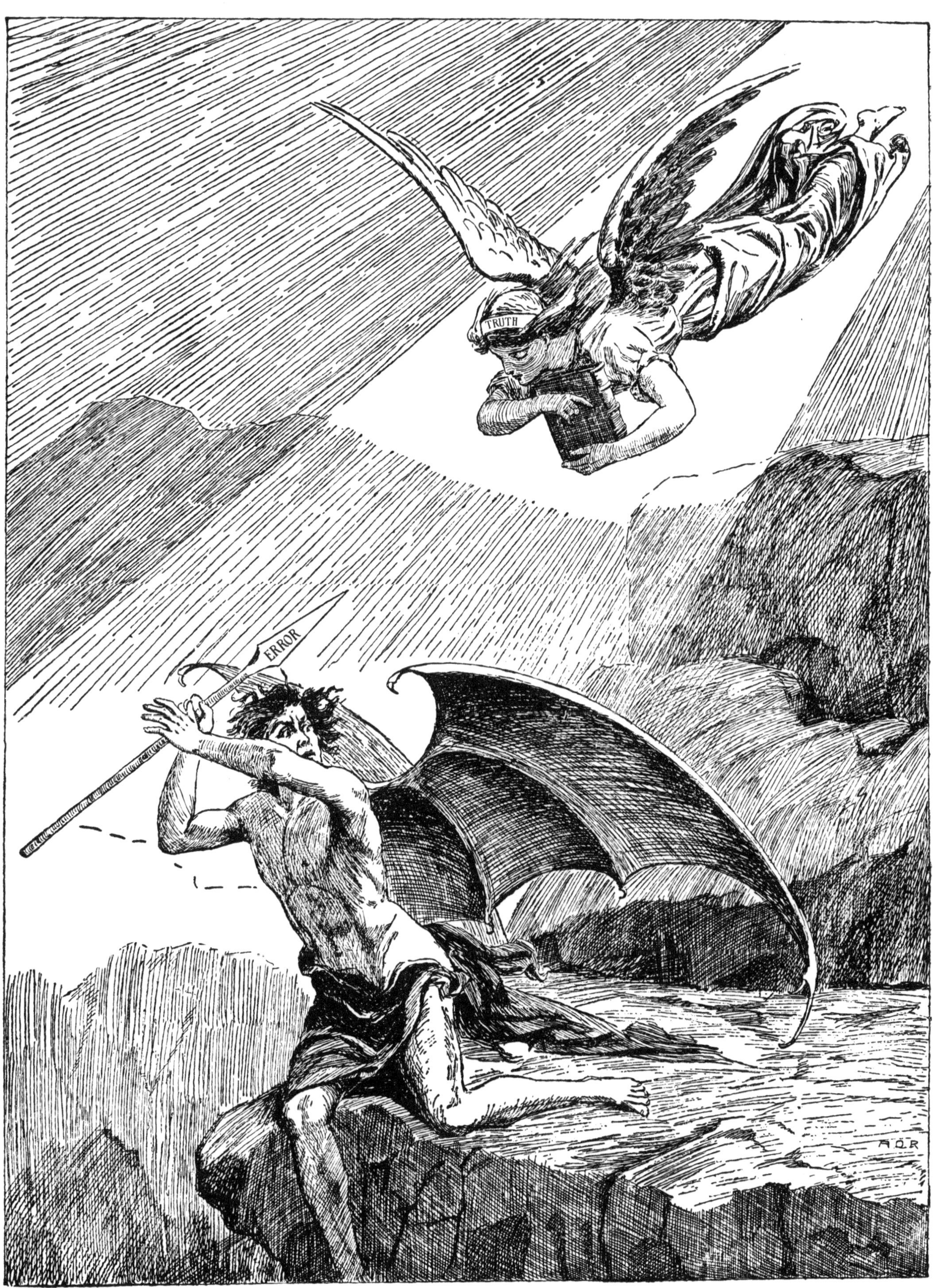
TRUTH
ERROR

Base Error Shrinks

Base error shrinks and trembles with affight,
When truth descends, arrayed in heavenly light.

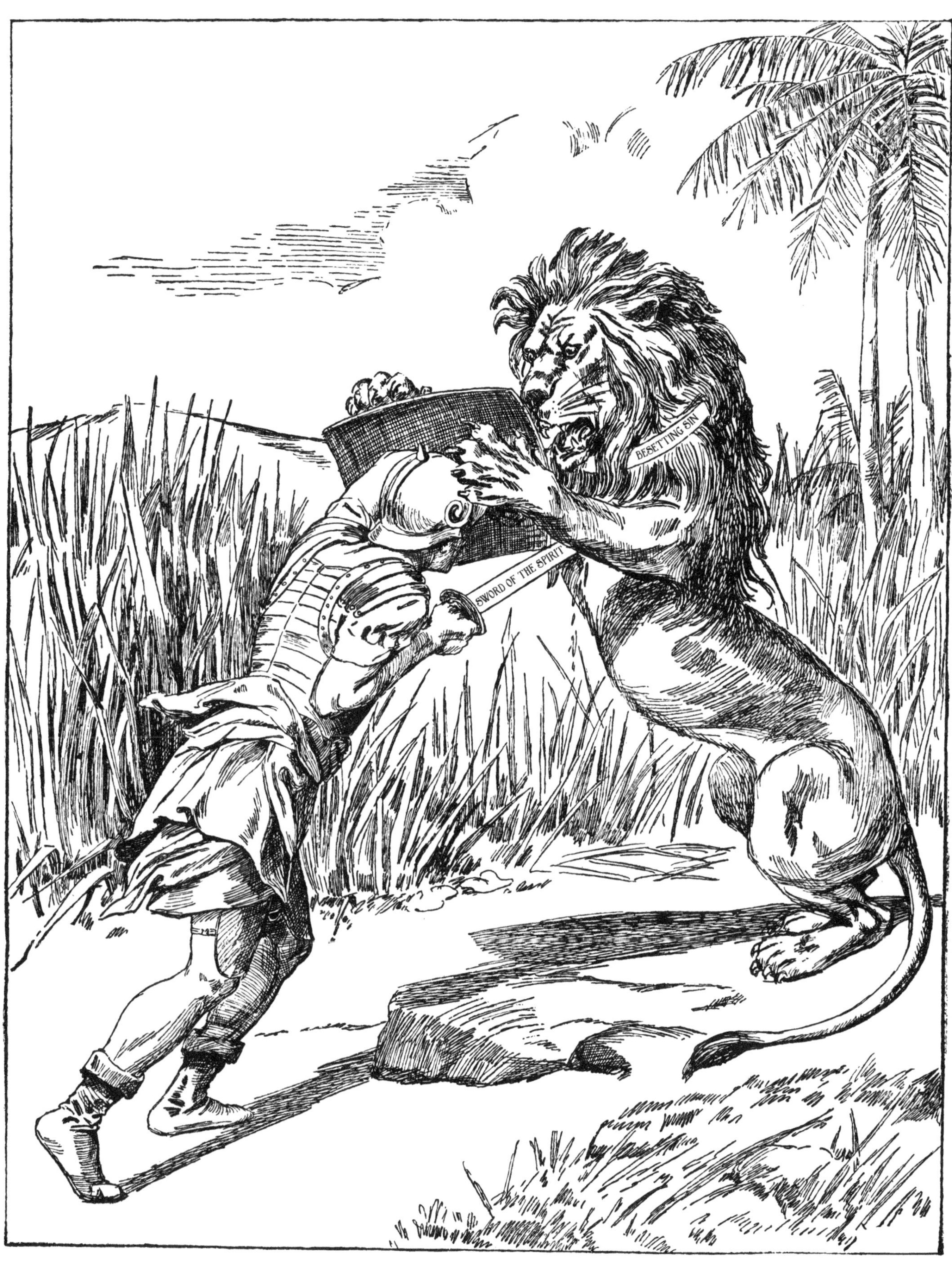
BESETTING SIN
SWORD OF THE SPIRIT

Fall Back Mighty Foe

Fall back, thou mighty foe, and bite the dust,
Slain by the Spirit's sharp and deadly thrust.

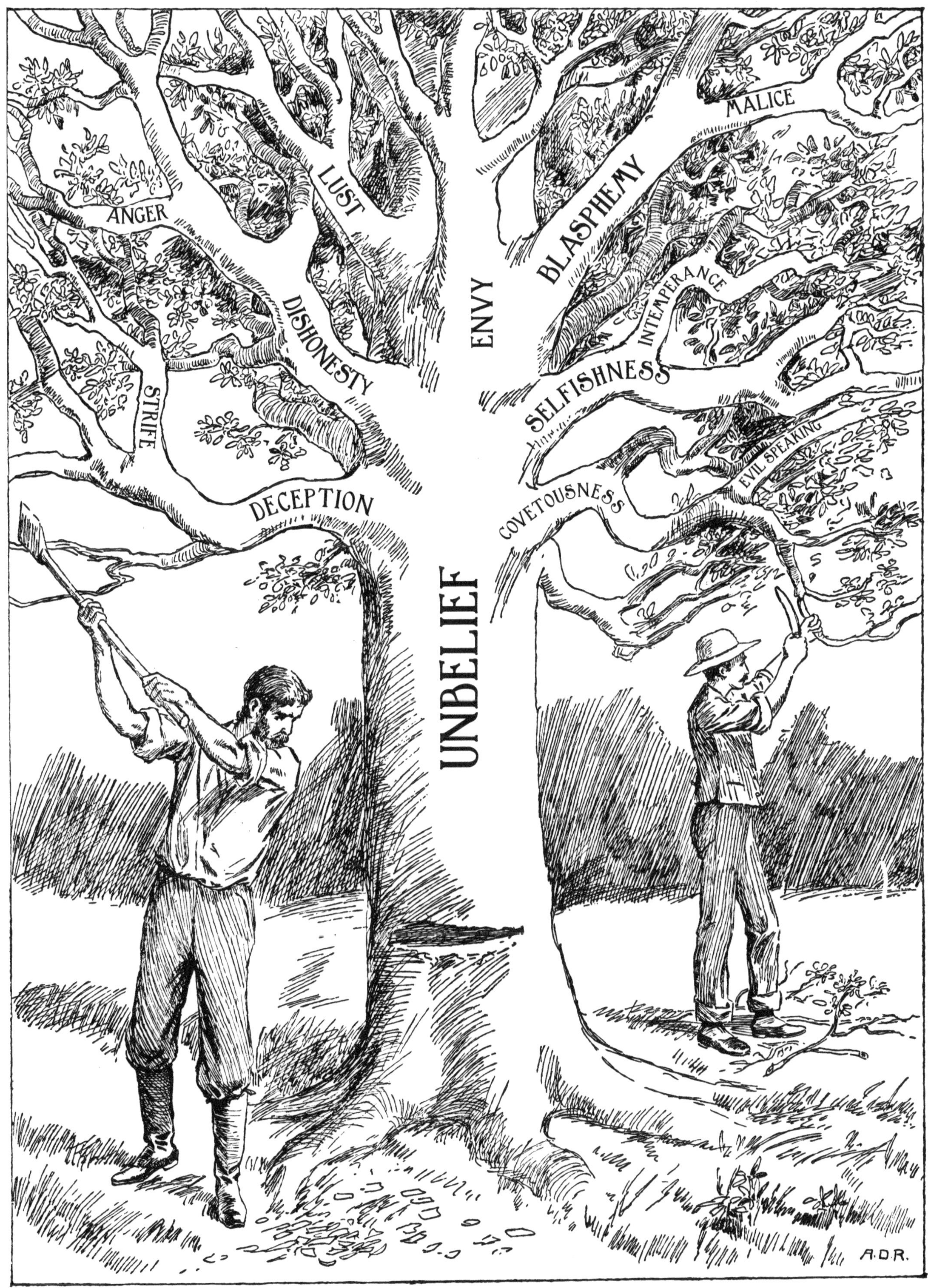
ANGER
LUST
ENVY
BLASPHEMY
MALICE
DISHONESTY
STRIFE
INTEMPERANCE
SELFISHNESS
EVIL SPEAKING
DECEPTION
COVETOUSNESS
UNBELIEF
A.D.R.

Tree of Unbelief

Vain task to merely clip the outer shoots,
Let the huge trunk be severed from the roots.

www.ingramcontent.com/pod-product-compliance
Lightning Source LLC
LaVergne TN
LVHW060620110826
845147LV00019B/1060

9781937564094